Lean

An Essential Guide to Lean Startup, Lean Six Sigma, Lean Analytics, Lean Enterprise, Lean Manufacturing, Agile Project Management, Kanban and Scrum

Contents

Part 1: Lean

The Ultimate Guide to Lean Startup, Lean Six Sigma, Lean Analytics, Lean Enterprise, Lean Manufacturing, Scrum, Agile Project Management and Kanban

Chapter 1: What is Lean?

Lean is a business strategy that is meant to eliminate waste so that the customer is happier and gets what they want. Whenever the customer is satisfied, the business can have more positive returns which are going to increase their sales and goodwill. Lean originated in the late 1990s to early 2000s with the automotive industry. The Japanese companies were dominating the American industry because they adopted the Lean business models and were focused on their customers instead of making money. It took America over a decade to regain the ground that they stole.

Traditional Lean business models include practices that allow the business to constantly improve their product, their quality management, and their just-in-time inventory systems. Each practice cuts back on wasteful spending and increases productivity and quality. Companies that follow the Lean business model make better quality products while making them cheaper, which in turn, makes shipping times smaller and the company more efficient in the long run.

For example, many companies focus on the customer when completing their business practices. But this did not happen all of the time. Henry Ford once said, about his cars, that customers could pick "any color so long as it is black." In other words, Henry Ford did not care what his customers wanted because he was making what he wanted and he was making money off of it. When we look back at what he did, his philosophy seems unwise, but unfortunately, this is how many companies used to act. As companies started realizing that this was not working for them, they began to focus more on their customer, and that is when the Lean business practices came into play.

Principles of Lean

Lean is a five-step process that you must think about before you can implement Lean techniques. You will find that these goals are not always going to be easy to implement, but with time, patience, and practice, you will be able to.

- Know the views of the customers on the basis of your products to specify your value.

- The steps of the value stream should be written down for every product family. What steps can you get rid of because they are not adding value to your product?

- The steps that create value should be in sequence tightly with the products so that the production line runs as smoothly as possible.

- While your flow is introduced, you should allow your customers to pull some value from another upstream activity.

- Once your value has been specified, then your value streams will be identified, and you can get rid of any wasted steps, which will introduce your flow and pull. To begin this process again, you have to continue until you reach a state of perfection, which will be the moment wherein there is no waste, and your perfect value is created.

Action Plan

Every company is going to face different challenges as they work on putting Lean into practice. There are a few vital steps that can be used to reduce resistance while spreading the proper learning and encouraging the right type of commitment needed to use Lean.

- *Locate a change agent:* Leaders will need to take responsibility when they are transforming with Lean.

- *Obtain Lean knowledge:* You can get knowledge about Lean from a consultant or someone who is experienced in Lean techniques and how it is going to be applied not as an isolated program but as a part of your system.

- *Seize the crisis:* You may find that you have to create a crisis in your company in order to start the transformation. If you are not in crisis mode, locate a Lean customer or focus on Lean competitors or supply who is going to make the demands needed to make you perform better.

- *Forget the grand strategy:* This is not going to be your main focus at the moment. Right now, you are going to be focusing on transforming your business.

- *Map value streams:* You need to start at the current state of your business and how much material and information is coming in. From there, you are going to be able to draw a Leaner future state so that everything that is coming in is implemented on a timetable.

- *Start now!* You are going to need to start now to achieve a transformation in your company.

- *Demand instant results:* You cannot wait for results. Your results need to be coming in now!

- *Expand your scope:* After you've been able to gain some momentum, link some of your improvements to the value streams by expanding your scope and moving past your offices and shops.

Channeling the Value Streams Through Creating the Organization

- Reorganize based on value streams and product family.

- Create functions for Lean promotion.

- Get rid of the excess people before promising that no one is going to lose their job since you are introducing Lean techniques.

- Plan your growth strategies.

- Get rid of anchor draggers.

- Even if you have fixed it once, you can always fix it again.

- It is okay if you take a step back, but it is not okay if you do not take any steps forward.

Installing Business Systems to Encourage Lean

- Create a deployment plan for your new policy.

- Set up a Lean accounting system.

- Pay your people based on their performance in your firm.

- Make sure your performance measurements are transparent to all employees.

- Teach Lean thinking to everyone.

- Make sure you have the proper tools before you start trying to inform people of your transformation.

Complete the Transformation

- Get your customers and suppliers to follow the procedures just laid out for you.

- Figure out a Lean global strategy.

- Convert starting at leadership and working your way down. Create strategies that are going to help you implement the new changes with all employees.

Transformation Framework

Everyone wants to transform, and that is what Lean is going to do for your business. You will be challenging yourself so that you are forced to reflect on how to improve your situation, your organization, and yourself. Everyone knows from experience that transformation is not easy.

No matter what your role is in the organization, you will be able to transform the company, but it is not going to be easy.

To better understand the nature of transformation, you have to understand what your mission is. By sharing the core values of your transformation, you are going to be helping others better understand what is going on, and by doing that, you will be narrowing the gap that is going to happen when you start your transformation.

By observing the efforts of your community, you will be able to understand what you are going to be working with which is going to help you have a successful transformation when it comes to situational approaches. At the same time, you will be establishing the key dimensions of your organization through a series of questions.

The questions are going to be fractal which means that the same questions can be applied to companies working on an enterprise level or those that are working on a smaller capacity. No matter how big your company is, Lean is going to force you to take responsibility and get deeper into each dimension of your company. Even though the transformation model has changed throughout the years, the experience is still situational because the nature of each question is going to represent a clean point of view. In the event that an organization does not address every question, the transformation is going to slow down or halt.

Questions

- What is the purpose of changing? What value are we providing or what problem are we attempting to solve?

- How can you improve your work?

- How are you building capability?

- What leadership programs need to be put into place so that we can support the transformation?

- What basic thinking or assumptions are going to comprise our current culture and what is driving our transformation?

Fundamentally, the process of a successful transformation is going to depend on the PDCA (plan-do-check-act) cycle for experimentation at each level all the time. When you are in the situation, you are only going to be focused on specific situations, and when you are grounded with a set of common principles that are situational when applied, you will be providing a rich opportunity for developing some profound wisdom. Lean is going to propose one set of point of view on each question. There are specific ways to approach each question so that you will yield greater success.

Common Questions

1. How does Lean apply to companies that are not manufacturing?

Because each core principle for Lean is going to be applied strongly, it can move past the shop floor. Many new breakthroughs are taking place because of Lean in services such as healthcare. It was John Shook, an LEI senior advisor, who once said, "TPS is described as a manufacturing system, but the thinking of TPS or Lean applies to any function. Whether you're dealing with 15,000 parts or 15 parts, or just providing a service, Lean works. It works because it is a way of thinking, a whole systems philosophy. Techniques aside, Lean thinking gives you a broad perspective on providing goods and services that go beyond the bottom line, beyond the stodgy principles of mass producing capitalism. It is a human system, customer-focused, and customer-driven wherein employees within and outside the workplace are also customers."

2. What are the usual errors when a company implements Lean?

To start using Lean, you have to make sure you are not looking at it as a headcount to get rid of anything or anyone that is not making you money. This is going to miss the Lean's purpose which is to create value by getting rid of waste. While your company improves its process, you will be empowered to reallocate your productive resources, so you can create work that is worthy of value. You should also remember that you should avoid the impulse you feel at the beginning to implement single Lean tools without understanding where they are going to fit in the bigger system. It is hard to avoid doing this with so many tools that are going to provide you with immediate payoffs. But, in the end, every Lean worker has to understand the *why* behind the tool, or else you will be losing its value. Those just starting out with Lean need to limit the scope of the first project so you can ensure that you are reaching success. Make sure that you have a leader that has a good attitude and deeper knowledge. Never be relaxed in your efforts of completing your transformation. One of the hardest things that you will face is the degree to which individual Lean success is going to uncover new problems.

3. How does Lean compare to other processes that can be used for improvement?

There are many differences in the schools that teach improvement processes. However, getting distracted by the competing schools should be cautioned. Veterans of every practice tend to get lost in the detailed arguments and all of the differences. However, by the end, your goal will still be the same as the other person. You will want the perfect value stream.

4. How can I encourage my associates and management to start practicing Lean?

This is a challenge that many businesses face, but you can do it! All you need to do is develop a Lean eye. In other words, be the change that you want to see. Do not expect your management to do something that you are not willing to do yourself!

5. *What are the best resources for Lean?*

Plenty of LEI workbooks and training can be found online. You can also find teachers of Lean that are willing to be hired so that they can help businesses reach their full potential.

Chapter 2: Lean Startup

Lean Startup is considered to be a proven method that can help businesses that are just starting out or assist products so that they can shorten the development cycle through the adaptation of business-hypothesis-driven experimentation, validated learning, and iterative product releases. The primary hypothesis for Lean is that if a startup company invests their time in building their products and services to meet the needs of their first customers, then they can reduce the market risks and work around the need for the large project funding as well as the expensive product launches that may fail.

Lean startup's method is based on Lean manufacturing which was made to streamline production processes started by Taiichi Ohno. He combined the principles that Henry Ford used in 1906 with the programs used by TWI in 1951. It took more than 15 years for Ohno to create a stable system that could be reproduced. The word Lean is used to describe this system when it was first published back in 1990 in the book *The Machine That Changed the World*.

Lean manufacturing believes that it is a waste of expenditure of resources if they are being used for anything other than to create a high-quality product for the customer. Lean manufacturing is always trying to find ways for waste to be eliminated. This system is going to focus on minimizing a company's inventory through the use of an assembly line. The Kanban cards are there to help signal when a business needs their inventory so they can increase their productivity. On top of that, it provides immediate quality control points where mistakes can be identified so they can be fixed as early as possible. This reduces the time spent on fixing faulty products. Another focus that is put on Lean management is to close the connection between suppliers, so they can understand what the customer wants.

There was an article written in the *Harvard Business Review* back in 2013 that described how Lean Startups were going to draw their inspiration from people like Rita Gunther McGrath and Ian C. MacMillan.

Definitions

1. *Minimum viable product (MVP):* this will be the version of the new product that enables a tech to collect as much as they can from the validated learning that they get from their last effort with their customer. Ultimately, the goal is going to be to test the business hypotheses so that entrepreneurs can start the learning process as quickly as possible.

2. *Continuous deployment (for software development only):* continuous deployment runs along the same lines as continuous delivery. It is a process where all the code that is written for applications will be instantly deployed into production which is going to help to reduce cycle times. There is a company that can deploy new code up to 50 times a day. This phrase was coined by Timothy Fitz.

3. *Split testing:* this is a trial where customers are offered several versions of the product at once. Examining the differences occurring on the two groups and measuring each version's impact using an actionable metric is the goal of this experiment. Split testing can be used incorrectly based on serial fashion because there is usually a group of users one week that see one version of the product, while the next week, they see another. This is going to undermine the validity of the results that you gather because there are external events that have the chance to influence their behavior from one time period to the next. Another way that split testing is commonly misused is when users are assigned to one of the product groups through the use of a non-random method.

4. *Actionable metrics:* actionable metrics are going to aid in the making of more informed decisions and the actions that are going to come from them. These measures are going to be different from vanity metrics because they do not paint the best picture possible when looking at the metrics of your business.

5. *Pivot:* pivots are structured course corrections that are done to test a hypothesis about a product, engine of growth, or strategy. One such example can be seen with Groupon. When this company first started, they were a platform known as The Point. But when they did not get any customers, the founders started a blog and launched their first coupon promotion. Even though they did not have much redemption, the founders saw how this slight change helped bring more people to their business because they can coordinate a group action. Now, Groupon is a billion-dollar business.

6. *Innovation accounting*: innovation accounting will refer to how entrepreneurs keep track of their accountability and how they can maximize their outcomes by measuring their progress and planning important milestones.

7. *Build – measure – learn:* this loop will put special emphasis on speed as part of the product development. The ability of the company to build a quality product quickly while measuring its effect on the market will determine its effectiveness. The phases of this loop are Idea – Build – Product – Measure – Data – Learn.

Tools for Lean Startup

Transforming your company cannot be done overnight, nor can it be done without the proper tools. The company that you run will depend on what tools are going to help you the most. Here, you will see some of the best tools to use while implementing Lean in your company.

- *Lean Canvas:* In the event that you are in the early stages of a startup, you are not going to want to waste time writing out a business plan. So, Lean Canvas takes your business model and turns it into a business plan. This tool adopts principles off of the business model you input through an easy to use web interface. You will have the option to create multiple canvases or collaborate and share with others in your business. You can also revisit your creation later. This is an adaptation of Business Model Toolbox.

- *Personapp:* Personapp helps you keep in mind to which you are creating your product for. You can create multiple personas per project, and you have the option to share and print out your personas.

- *Unassumer:* This is a new addition to the Lean startup tools, and it has proven to be quite valuable. It was created by Brant Cooper, a customer development expert. Unassumer helps businesses to learn what the customers really want and puts their prospects into a scoring system so that you can get the data you can use instantly to target the proper market.

- *Kiss Insights:* Your customers now have a way to tell you what they need out of what you are offering them. All you need to do is ask your customer a question or a series of questions, and the customer will see it come up from the bottom of your site. This is a place for them to offer you feedback to better your company.

- *Survey.io:* You can use this tool to test products so you can find the market that fits your product. You will be able to use their template to create a survey, or you can use Kiss Insights to create your own.

- *Google Apps:* It is an assortment of free or cheap tools on Google you can use with a Lean Startup. Docs allow you to create spreadsheets and presentations. You will use them as you would Microsoft office, but you will hack them, so they fit your needs better.

- *Unbounce:* With Unbounce, you can create a landing page and do split testing. This will take out the pain of creating a landing page because HTML is not needed. This way, you can also quickly test your new product idea.

- *WuFoo:* WuFoo creates forms that can be placed on your site without having a developer involved. It has a user-friendly interface, so you can manage your forms and keep track of conversions and analytics.

- *Usertesting.com:* You cannot replace face-to-face tests, but usertesting.com can be used to pinpoint usability at an early stage. Their tests test anything that is in its early stages including web apps. Your product will be reviewed and an audio commentary provided while they are using it.

- *Silverback:* With this piece of software you can record live usability tests through a built-in webcam so you can watch and share with colleagues later. Along with recording, you can record screen activity to track every stage of your test.

- *Intercom:* Here you will have a place for all of your teams to communicate with each other and with customers. You can place Intercom on your website, mobile apps, or use email communication.

- *Buzzsumo:* With Buzzsumo, you can get marketing intelligence so you can improve your efforts. You can also analyze to see what product performs best for a variety of topics. Locate your key influencers that can help promote your content.

- *Yoast:* Yoast SEO used to be called WordPress SEO and is still a plugin that can be used with WordPress users. It includes everything from previews to page analysis so that you can optimize your website better.

- *Canva:* This startup tool provides you with all the tools you need to turn your ideas into brilliant designs. It works for everything from blogs to Facebook and more.

- *StockSnap:* Here you can find beautiful free photos that you can use for your graphics.

Lean Startup Business Plan

One problem that most people face is creating a business plan that suits what they are trying to do. To have a successful business, you must have a business plan that you can follow and show your investors. Having a plan to follow will also keep you from going off and changing your business in the middle of what you are trying to do.

- *Start your business plan:* Startups have to deal with a lot of uncertainty like establishing principles of management that may not be suited for what they are doing or cannot foster the spirit of innovation. When you start a business, you will need to look at the climate that the economy is in, but it is not a bad idea to start your business with Lean so that you can get a leg up on your competition.

Lean business plans address what challenges you will face as an entrepreneur. By creating a plan, you will be preparing yourself to deal with the unexpected through the process of measuring, building, and learning. With this process, you will be able to reduce or avoid any perils that many startups tend to face. Thanks to the advances in technology, we have been given every tool needed to improve the capabilities for production. However, many startups set themselves up for failure since they lack the scientific approach and discipline to create early-stage venture management. The failure comes when jobs are lost.

Lean Startup business plans are going to address every area of business that is still in its early stages. These areas include the development of product, conception, and the measurement of progress as well as the structure of the organization. If you are an entrepreneur, you will need to determine if the market is looking for what you are selling.

•	*Define your vision:* Cultivating your entrepreneurship is one of the biggest responsibilities that the upper management is going to have. Management needs to be headed in the direction where they can handle any uncertainties that come up. Management should be able to guide the product from just an idea all the way to the production stage, even when uncertainty comes when starting your own business. The stage where you define your business in the Lean business plan will be where you develop the vision that you have. This strategy is to implement your plans so that you can get your vision further than before. The business strategy that you use will include a number of elements, each of which is going to include researching the market that you are planning to serve. You will have to alter your measurements so that you can learn what you should and should not. However, your vision is going to stay the same.

•	*Learning:* Learning is not going to stop once you've developed your business idea. You will need to figure out how to make it work in the real world so that you can get it out of the conception stage and make it so that it is a working product. It is vital that you understand the parts of your business plan that are going to benefit you in reaching your goal and which you can let go of. When you can do this, you are going to find that you will be the one who decides if your business succeeds or fails. Everyone who invests money in your operation, and those who are working for you, are going to depend on you to lead them to success. So, you have to learn to face the facts about the prospects for your organization and assess the results of your current business strategy.

•	*Experiment with your idea:* You are not going to learn anything if you are not willing to step outside of your comfort zone. Experimenting is going to be a blind toss out of ideas to see what works and what does not. The science that is behind the experimenting is going to involve testing theories in the real world. The theories you test will come from the vision that you set up and wrote in your business plan to work with real customers. This testing will provide you with the information that you need to make concrete decisions. This information cannot be obtained without practical experiments though.

•	*Leap of faith:* This is an essential step if you want to move forward with your plan. The point of experimenting is to ensure you are not taking your leap of faith blindly. While you start your own business, the biggest questions you will be asking yourself are if you can build your product and if the market is going to want your product? When the answer is yes to both of these questions, only then will you be successful. You are going to fail. You have to fail or else you are not going to be able to take your leap of faith and push your business plan past the idea stage.

- *Testing your idea:* At this point, you are going to take your second leap of faith. Here, we are going to assume that you have found customers and you are going to start giving them pieces of your product to test and see if they are going to be successful. When you can meet the demands of a small market, then it is going to prepare you for the bigger launch. You can always give your first customers a free trial to see how well it goes over on a larger market.

- *Measure results:* What is your testing telling you? You are going to need to find an effective way to analyze the data that you have gathered from your testing. You need to implement the means of discovering what your customers like and what they don't like. The method of measurement is going to be different depending on the type of business you are running. Learn what metrics you need to pay attention to and the methods that you use to get them. Should your metrics indicate a negative response, then you will need to figure out what your customer is really wanting.

- *Pivot – how and when:* Pivoting means you will be changing your business strategy without changing your vision. What is going to happen if your measurements are negative? Or if your testing informs you that no one is going to buy your product? You have to adapt your vision to meet the various needs of the market. Taking these measurements, you will form a new approach to your business. The business needs to be Agile to handle dramatic shifts in the method you use should the metrics dictate that one be necessary.

- *Working with small batches:* For small startups, the speed of production is vital. It has to seem as if it is counterintuitive as you produce your product in small batches so that it is more efficient than producing in large ones. Think of the first batch as one step in the production process that has to be completed before you can move on. The larger the batch, the more risks you are going to run into with delays and the more difficult it will be for you to make revisions. A small batch will allow the whole process to be completed quicker. The faster the production process, the faster you are going to find the problems and remedy them, so you are effectively using your resources.

- *Sustaining growth:* You want your business to grow, and there are three ways that you can start to see growth in your startup. The first one is through continual returns of satisfied customers, the next is word of mouth, and the last is advertising and sales. When satisfied customers return to your business, you will be exceeding your new custom acquisition. The next is viral growth, and it is the most important measurement because a new customer can be brought in with each user that gets their hands on your product. The last is going to cost you money and can be helpful or hurtful depending on how you promote your product.

- *Adapting to new circumstances:* What it boils down to is that you cannot expect that you are not going to have to adjust your plan because of something that is thrown at you. You will have to have a business plan that is set up so that you can adjust should life throw you a curveball. Adapting to new situations will show you how you can adapt to things like a change in the market, or new demands from your customer.

- *Foster innovation*: Innovation is not limited to those companies just starting out. It is beneficial to the companies that are established as well. Nurturing and encouraging the attitude of an entrepreneur in your management is going to help to create a culture that is innovative as well as sustained.

Lean Startup Kanban Approach

As you just learned, a Lean Startup is going to be about innovation. Lean is a philosophy that has been tested in the field so that it is a plan that will minimize the failure of a company while increasing its chances of success. Lean Startup borrows a variety of practices that are found in Kanban and Lean manufacturing when it comes to focusing on adaption and execution of your business plan. Kanban is considered a powerful method that supports visuals for work instead of written words. This can be one of the best strategies to be used with startups because it helps to characterize your work based on constant adjustments and a quick feedback loop. As you use Kanban, you are going to focus on visualizing the work that you are currently doing so that you can keep your workflow smooth and learn from your mistakes to reduce your cycle time. It is easy to get started with Kanban because you will be using a whiteboard that has sticky notes placed on it or other online solutions that allow your team to visualize the process.

Example

When using a Kanban board, the work progression will go left to right. Whenever a new task is dropped in your lap, you will place it in the to-do column based on how important it is.

How Kanban Can Help You

As stated, startups tend to face many challenges, but Kanban is the perfect solution because it allows the startup to learn and pull more value out of their process.

Teams that use Kanban are more likely to make discoveries about their workflow that can improve their development over those companies that do not use Kanban. These improvements are important to any business, but with startups, it can be a matter of if they can continue going through their process, or if they are going to "die" before they can get off the ground. So, with Kanban, startups are going to be more prone to improve constantly instead of becoming stagnant.

Kanban helps to streamline flow while limiting the work in progress so that the valued product can be delivered faster and regularly which makes the entire system more efficient.

Becoming a Lean Startup with the Kanban Tool

Kanban is a tool that helps with the visual for Lean Startups. Kanban supports real-time collaboration, and this is done so that teams can get work done faster. It also provides online advanced Kanban boards with a large range of features you can customize including power-ups. Kanban tools provide insightful analytics and metrics when it comes to monitoring and improving a project's performance.

Questions

- *Who is going to use Lean Startups?*

Innovators and entrepreneurs are going to be the primary companies that use Lean Startups. These techniques can be seen in corporations like GE when it comes to redefining product development and department functions. Lean Startup principles are going to be used to transform their ideas into something that they can market. The government uses Lean to deliver services by breaking through the barriers of bureaucracy.

- *Is it only used for startups?*

No! As the world continues to change, companies are coming to realize that they have to keep up with the evolving market. Eric Ries said in his book, *The Startup Way,* "In today's marketplace of uncertainty, whoever learns fastest wins." Therefore, the principles of entrepreneurial management are going to be applied across all sectors no matter how big the company is.

- *Is Lean Startup used just to make products?*

No. Lean Startups are less about building your product and more about defining and supplying the proper amount in the appropriate time. Lean Startups are going to take advantage of the energy that entrepreneurs have for new ideas and spread that energy out to create an internal process design. These startups can usually find a foothold in product development, but it is a fundamental tenant to any innovative design.

- *What industries are using Lean Startups?*

There are not many companies that cannot use Lean Startup. If you are supplying something of value to a customer, then you can use Lean Startup.

- *What hardware do you need for a Lean Startup?*

Lean Startups were developed in a Lean startup in Silicon Valley. The methodology has gone beyond the company, but Lean Startups have also gone beyond technology products. The Lean startup methods will provide new ways for businesses to supply customers value without too much risk or expense that can be seen in traditional product development processes.

Chapter 3: Lean Six Sigma

Definition of Six Sigma

Six Sigma is a business method that is not only defined but also disciplined in order to increase the customer's satisfaction along with increasing profitability through the streamlining of operations, improving quality, and getting rid of any defects throughout the entire organization.

So what makes up Six Sigma?

• *Business strategies:* With the Six Sigma methods, businesses can strategize a plan of action while driving an increase in revenue as well as cutting costs and planning improvements.

• *Vision:* Senior management will be able to create a vision that is free from defects while investing for the organization's positive environment.

• *Benchmark:* Six Sigma is about the improvement of process metrics. After the process has reached a state of stability, you will have to use Six Sigma in improving the new metrics. For example, you run a delivery service, and you improve your service times from 60 minutes to 45 minutes with Six Sigma. After you have established your services at 45 minutes, you will use Six Sigma again to improve the cycle from 45 minutes to 30 minutes. This will be your benchmark.

• *Goal:* With Six Sigma, organizations will stick to their goals and work to achieve them over the time period that they set. With the right use of the methodology, you will learn how to achieve these goals.

• *Statistical measure:* The methodology is what Six Sigma is all about. Statistical analysis is about identifying the root cause of the issue. On top of that, Six Sigma is going to calculate the process using a sigma unit.

- *Robust methodology:* Six Sigma is the only method that can be used on the market today with a documentation strategy for problem-solving. If you use it properly, you will be creating improvements that are bulletproof, and they will give you a high yield.

DMAIC

DMAIC is a method that is going to be used when you are solving issues that lie behind Lean Six Sigma. There are five measures for DMAIC: define, measure, analyze, improve, and control.

Choose the proper project: Before you can begin your improvement process, you have to pick a project that is a good candidate for improvement so you can set yourself up for success. A few good projects for improvement are:

- Projects that have obvious problems in their existing process.

- Projects that have collectible data and results that show that it needs improvement.

- Any project that has the potential to reduce the lead time or any defects that will save money or improve productivity.

There will be obstacles that can be found in smooth operations for every business, and Lean Six Sigma is going to offer guidelines for you to pick the proper projects at the correct time. Your improvement teams can use DMAIC so you can refine the projects and deliver results.

Now, let's look at the DMAIC process.

Define

What is the problem that you are attempting to fix? It is the first phase of Lean Six Sigma process. It is during this phase that the project team will create a project charter which is a map of the process so that you can begin to understand the needs of your customers. This phase cannot be skipped because it is when the team outlines the project's focus for themselves and leadership.

Steps

- Figure out the problem with a problem statement.

- Define your goal through your goal statement.

- Define the process with a process map.

- Define what your customer wants.

- Inform your team of the project's process.

Tools

1. A3
2. project charter

3.   tree diagram

4.   SIPOC

5.   relationship map

6.   value stream map

7.   stakeholder analysis

8.   voice of the customer translation matrix

9.   swimlane map

Measure:

How is your process performing right now? How big is the problem? Measurements are vital throughout the lifespan of the project. While a team collects data, they are going to focus on the process as well as measuring what customers want. That means that there will be two focuses. The first one is reducing the lead time as well as improving the quality. In this phase, you will be redefining the measurement definitions as you determine the current performance or the baseline of your process.

Steps

- Figure how the process is currently performing

- Create a plan that enables you to collect data

- Make sure your data is reliable

- Get a baseline for your data

- Update your charter

Tools

- data collection plan

- project charter

- check sheet

- operational definitions

Analyze:

What is causing the problem? This phase is often skipped over, but without analysis, teams tend to jump to solutions before they can find out what is truly causing the issue. The result is a team that implements a solution but finds that they are not solving the issue. This ends up being a waste of time and resources while you end up causing more issues to arise. The best idea is for your teams to brainstorm what could be the cause of your problem before you brainstorm solutions. Why are these issues coming up and how do we work to prove or disprove why they are there?

Steps

- Examine the processes you are using
- Display your data on a graph
- Look for what could be causing your problem
- Verify what is causing your problem
- Update your charter

Tools

- charter
- value stream map
- root cause hypothesis
- value added flow analysis
- 5 whys
- run charts
- fishbone diagram
- histograms
- box plots
- Pareto charts

Improve:

How can you mitigate the root cause of your issue? After you have figured out what the root cause is, then you need to find a solution. This phase is where you will brainstorm solutions and try out different solutions to see which one works. You will need to collect data to ensure that you are getting the proper improvement. Structured improvement is going to help lead to innovation and more elegant solutions to improve your baseline measurement and ultimately the experience your customer has.

Steps

- Brainstorm a solution
- Select practical solutions

- Develop maps based on different solutions

- Pick the best solution

- Implement the solution

- Measure the improvement

Tools

- implementation plan

- brainstorming

- pilot checklists

- benchmarking

- PDCA/PDSA

- classic Lean movements

- swimlane map

- weighted criteria matrix

- value stream map

- impact effort matrix

Control:

How can you sustain the improvement that you've been making? Since you have fixed the problem, you need to measure the gains that you are making. In the control phase, your team will be focused on creating a plan that can help to monitor the success while also updating anything that is not working in the event that there is a dip in the performance.

Steps

1. Make sure your process is being managed and monitored

2. Document your improvement

3. Apply your improvement to other areas

4. Share your success

5. Keep your improvement up with Lean principles

Tools

1. gallery walks

2. control plan

3. innovation transfer opportunities

4. control chart

5. documentation

6. monitoring and response plan

Six Sigma process disciplines

Document your process: By documenting your process, you will be helping your team to define the measures and controls of your business processes. Six Sigma along with Lean tools is useful when documenting your process.

By documenting your progress, you will be ensuring:

1. That everyone can understand your current processes, so you can measure the performance of future projects.

2. Standardizing your processes across your entire company.

3. Allowing your business continuity in the event that you experience non-availability of key subject matter experts.

Process improvement: Improving processes will be an effort that you use when identifying the highest priority problems in your business. You will need teams that are trained to identify these problems and tackle them. Thanks to the methods of DMAIC, you can identify your problems and work to solve them.

Process improvement (Lean): There are two different factors that you must consider when working with Lean. The first one is non-value added, and the other is value added. Your customer will be looking for value which means that, on the first trial, you are doing the right thing. Whenever a value is added, that means that the product is adding value to the process. If it is not adding value to the process, then it will need to be removed.

Six Sigma Focus

Six Sigma has a formula that you will follow when you are working with it. This formula is:

$Y = f(X) + E$

Y will be your results that you want from your process. This will depend on X and will be the dependent factor.

X is the representation of the input factor that will result in Y. You may have several Xs, and each will be an independent factor.

E shows errors that may appear or any uncertainty that is surrounding X and how they will affect the outcome.

In simpler terms, input variables will change the function when combined with an error so that an output can be formed. Y will come from a function of X. To figure out your output, you need to transform your process (f) with your inputs.

For instance, if you are forming a thin sheet of metal, the metal will go through several processes. The input variables are the chemicals that go into creating that metal sheet. The raw materials will be known as the Xs while the mixing of these materials will be f, ultimately, your metal sheet is Y. E can be an error that is introduced into the process.

Or, if we examine the delivery example, a few reasons that you are not able to meet the 30-minute delivery time is because the driver does not know where the address is, there is heavy traffic, or the delivery was not prepared on time. So, your delivery time will be Y, and the reasons why the delivery was not on time are X. Focus on X and not Y.

As you go through a Six Sigma project, your focus needs to be on identifying the cause/s and getting rid of it/them. The result will improve once you have dealt with the issues correctly. So, ensure your teams are focusing not on the end result but the causes.

Six Sigma Roles and Responsibilities

Six Sigma is split up into two segments: Project leadership and Initiative leadership.

Even though those are the two most important segments, Six Sigma will require these roles as well.

1. yellow belt (YB)
2. black belt (BB)
3. deployment leadership
4. green belt (GB)
5. champion
6. master black belt (MBB)

Deployment leader

1. Group leaders must follow the Six Sigma, and they can do so by:
2. Taking part in Six Sigma activities.
3. Creating objectives where Six Sigma can be used to achieve the goals.
4. Creating an environment that ensures success. Success will be closely tied to how much time the leaders invest in their business and the use of Six Sigma.
5. Provide a goal that will be driven by Six Sigma on every level.
6. Six Sigma and roll-out plans will need to be planned for the whole organization.

7. Working with MBB will be used to identify the organization's vision and mission statement.

8. You should hire a team of people that are experienced in MBB and BBs.

Benefits of Being a Deployment Leader

1. A deployment leader can help the organization in developing a Six Sigma culture while still helping in nurturing a culture of constant progress.

2. By driving the Six Sigma methods in your organization, your deployment leader will have the power to run the company to its fullest potential.

Champion

The project champions are the sponsors but also the management for the business, and they are going to be considered the Six Sigma team's high priority. Champions play a crucial role in owning the processes that the business uses which means that they have to ensure these process improvements can be sustained.

This level will usually manage the green belts (GBs), so they have to understand any of the challenges that these GBs will have tied to them. On top of that, they will be working with MBBs and BBs to make sure that these areas of business are fully established which means that they have to implement a vision that is long-term and can work with Six Sigma across the board.

Details Tied to the Champion

1. *Training:* Sponsors must be trained in all parts of Six Sigma.

2. *Support:* There should be a visual support of Six Sigma, MBB, BB, and GBs so that the proper resources are obtained for the project to be finished.

3. *Scope:* A clear scope needs to be set for every project. The project needs to be defined clearly while the scope kept between four and six months. The progress should be monitored to make sure that the scope stays inside the bounds that were originally laid out.

4. *Expectations:* The bar should be set high when it comes to the result's value. Goals may not be sub-optimized. Six Sigma has shown that value can be delivered beyond what is initially estimated. When your goals are less aggressive, the results match.

5. *Facts:* Do not be afraid to challenge the experts on the knowledge that they hold and any basis that they may have for their conclusions.

6. *Involvement:* Champions need to interact with the teams so they can take part in the problem-solving sessions as resources are allocated. You should plan on spending two hours weekly with your project team.

7. *Hand over:* Sponsors are the ones in charge of ensuring that the business will be responsible for the execution to look at seeing if they are delivering the value that was

pointed out during the control phase. This usually will mean that there will need to be a specific individual who is going to take ownership of the project metrics and their delivery to the rest of the team.

8. *Results:* The champions and Six Sigma mentors will work with the business controls to make sure that all of the results from the project will achieve the goal of the corporation.

The Champion's Benefits

1. Champions will create a portfolio that shows their skills from projects focused on quality, customer satisfaction, cost, and service. This provides a visual for the process while also showcasing the champion's abilities and what they can do on a variety of projects.

2. They set the improvement's directions for the business. Champions are the ones who link the organizational priorities to the project's benefits.

Master Black Belt (MBB)

MBBs are those that will be responsible for translating the goals from the upper management to everyone else who will be there helping make the goals a reality. MBBs will primarily work with deployment teams. They will also help to command the Six Sigma skills development needed for the GBs, BBs, and all other general associates. This team will have to make sure that they are paying close attention to the quality, sustainability, and value of the Six Sigma projects.

MBBs work together to reach the success of the divisions Six Sigma effort by coordinating and leading activities that will be key in the cross-division value streams. They also ensure that there is a culture valuing creativity in the workplace and that their team still makes an effort to challenge the existing social structure and value.

Deliverables

1. Project executions and the removal of roadblocks

2. Roll-out plans and Six Sigma strategies for the organization

3. Cross-functional leadership

4. Management of projects

5. Achieving desired lean Six Sigma results

Benefits

1. MBB grows as the ladder goes up and eventually turns into the chief quality officer.

2. MBB sets up a culture for Six Sigma starting at the bottom.

3. A BB can become a MBB after proper mentoring.

Black Belt (BB)

BBs are leaders (either part time or full time) that will mentor those in the business as well as the GBs. BBs will be responsible for executing a specific set of projects as well as ensuring that these results are written down and given to the champions as other changes are sustained. BBs also impart their knowledge of Six Sigma on a part-time and full member.

BBs are presumed to be the ones to cultivate and nurture an open and honest environment. They challenge the status quo when it is proper for them to, and they seek to share their ideas across the entire organization.

Deliverables

1. Share practices

2. Six Sigma strategy and roll out a plan

3. Teach green belts

4. Execute projects

5. Results from Six Sigma projects

6. Guide project resources while getting rid of project level barriers

7. Project and team structuring

Benefits

1. BBs are trained to improve results so that the organization can use their statistical analysis and Six Sigma tools. This is why they have a lucrative path which ranges from business analysts to process improvement experts.

2. BBs have the responsibility of moving the improvements of the process for the organization to the next level.

Green Belt (GB)

They are the engine of the on-going project of Six Sigma. While BBs support the efforts and implement changes, GBs are only temporary project leaders, and they are responsible for managing interfaces, making sure the results are sustainable, asking for help when it is needed, picking the project, and even leading the team.

In the end, using the work problems, green belts will translate the value of Six Sigma.

Deliverables

1. Sharing best practices

2. Project execution

3. Six Sigma results

4. Team and project structuring

Benefits

1. When it comes to self-career, GBs will get exposure to senior management because of the virtue of their projects, which means they will have the chance to make a difference in their organization.

2. GBs will have the authority of their own so that work gets done effectively and efficiently. This is vital because it helps to build processes and improve structure for every process.

Yellow belt (YB)

A YB will be a part-time or full-time project-specific resource that provides information that will make the process better as well as the knowledge that they have to help sustain gains that are made. They will have the project's co-ownership with the experts of Six Sigma and are considered to be in charge of the work's quality that has been put out and the results that come back from it.

The YB team plays a vital role when it comes to translating all the process gains into other areas of the organization once the project has been finished.

Deliverables

1. YBs use the best sharing practices and Lean tools for smaller improvements of the process they are responsible for

2. YBs will only have basic knowledge of what Six Sigma is

3. A YB is going to participate as a subject matter expert or as a main team member on DMAIC projects. They support black and green belts when developing process maps, gathering data, or changing simulations

4. YBs are not going to lead projects on their own

Benefits

1. For any project, a YB will be the person who is the subject matter expert of their process and will have a basic knowledge of Six Sigma. They are a spoke on the wheel and will be there driving the Six Sigma processes to closure based on their expertise. Organizations are going to benefit from having the right YB for their project.

2. When it comes to self-career, YBs are going to get more exposure by channeling their subject knowledge where it can improve processes as well as yield benefits that can be understood by all.

Best practices

Every Six Sigma effort that is successful will have practices that are similar to other projects. Even if you have been using Six Sigma for a while, you need to look at what you've done for other projects and figure out what has been most effective for you.

1. *Set stretch goals:* Six Sigma should not be used for just any manager or individual who wants to enhance their process' output periodically. No, this is for those who want to improve their organization by miles instead of inches.

Six Sigma has been proven to create improvement, but it can only be reached when combining tools with stretch goals and Six Sigma methods. Stretch goals are going to be aggressive and optimistic. Stretch goals usually account for 70% of the improvement that happens in organizations. For instance, your business profit margin is around 7%, and you want a margin of 11.9% which is the 70% increase you are searching for. You will set up a stretch goal that will help you reach that 70% increase.

Another way to look at it is to set a stretch target that benchmarks yourself against your competition. Benchmarks are levels of performance that are reached by some of the best companies, functions, and processes. If someone else is going to be able to do it, why can't you? Look at the Toyota Company. It took them time to benchmark the introduction of a new vehicle, and they did it in for their hybrid car around 24 but it also presented challenges technically that went far from the traditional cars.

2. *Tangible results:* Most organizations with Six Sigma can lower their costs by 30%. However, at the same time, their revenues increase by more than 10%. For these returns to be realized, every project of Six Sigma has to be linked to a tangible result. These results will be measured through financial returns which used to be tracked and rolled up into a financial return that has been hallmarked by Six Sigma. But if you cannot link your project to a tangible measurement while you track their financial impact, it will naturally move away from its financial potential.

In some cases, these projects will not focus on revenue enhancement or cost reduction. Instead, strategic objectives that are set for the organization will be its main focus. So, if your objective is to increase brand awareness when finishing a project, then you will have a hard time quantifying your improvements. However, should it enable key strategies of the company, then your effort in the project is worth it.

3. *Determine your outcomes:* Your input determines each outcome. The outgrowth of this principle is that you actively control and adjust your inputs to get your desired outcomes.

4. *Thoughts before actions:* Many people jump into action so they can solve a problem without thinking about the solution. This often happens because they are confusing action

with effectiveness which causes the problem to continue to grow or provides a solution that does not fully solve the problem.

The DMAIC method encourages the team to move their concentration to determine the cause of the problem from solving the problem so that they can prepare the appropriate solution. Every project normally starts first with identifying the problem and knowing the solution's objectives. Verifying the current system or process' performance is the next step. The outputs, conditions, and the inputs will be analyzed next. Once all of these steps have been completed, an optimal solution will improve the process.

5. *Trust the data:* Without any information, the basis of your decisions will be on wishful thinking and opinions. But data allows you to look at the information objectively and pick the best ideas and solutions along with coming up with alternatives. Your decisions have to be based on the data even though it is not easy. Data will require you to put aside your judgment and personal bias so you can look at the facts.

6. *Minimize variation:* Many people think that the only basis of success is the single numbers like the monthly cost of running the department, the rate of returns, or the average yield on the production line. However, the reality is that the variation of these numbers, despite the fact that they could be at an acceptable level, can cause more damage than the actual number.

For example, it is good to have a high average number of orders. But the numbers you see each day will vary based on the kind of day you have, which means that the company could have an excess of staff and equipment on some days, but this should happen so that you are not harming your company on the days that you have a better day than the last. Variation will be there in all of the products that you make or the plans that you design.

7. *Align key goals:* An important factor for a successful Six Sigma project is to ensure that the projects are aligned with the objectives of the organization and key goals. The efforts of Six Sigma will be successful and will last because the projects will concentrate on ensuring that the organization moves towards its goals.

8. *Celebrate your success:* Six Sigma starts out small, but ultimately, it grows and can include the entire company! You will see staggering financial returns, and you should celebrate that success. Even if your success starts out small, those small victories will add up in the end!

Chapter 4: Lean Analytics

What is Lean analytics? The core idea behind Lean analytics is to know the kind of business that you are running, and at what stage you are working with so you can track and optimize the One Metric That Matters in your startup. If you repeat this process, you will have the power to overcome most of the risks that companies have to deal with in the early stages of their projects. You will also be avoiding premature growth, and you will be building on a foundation of true needs, happy customers, and well-defined solutions.

As you have learned, one thing that every startup has to have if they want to be successful is that they need to achieve real focus which means that they must have the discipline to maintain that focus. There is a chance that businesses will succeed by being focused, but it is going to be an accident because most of the time, you will be trying to figure out what to do and the lessons that you learn will be harder to understand and your victories harder to achieve. Therefore, it is vital that you have some sort of focus.

Having focus does not mean that you have to focus on a single metric from the moment that the project is born. Instead, you should have a metric that you put above all the other metrics. Looking at it in simpler terms, Lean Startups are about getting a business to focus on the proper metrics at the proper time ensuring that they have the proper mindset when working towards their goal.

The author of *The Lean Startup*, Eric Ries, talks about the three engines that will drive a company's growth. The first is the sticky engine, the second the viral engine, and the last, the paid engine. Ries cautions that every successful company is going to have all three engines, but it is better to focus on one engine at a time.

For example, you want to make your product sticky for those that are using it first so that it can grow virally which will then help to grow revenue.

Looking at the world of data and analytics, you will need to select a single metric that is important to the stage you are currently on for your startup. This is known as the One Metric That Matters (OMTM).

OMTM is a number that you will put all of your focus into above everything else because it is vital to the stage your startup is on. You will need to examine the customer lifetime value even though this is not going to be helpful when you are attempting to validate a problem, but it is a metric that you should focus on when you are trying to find the right market for your project.

No matter what stage you are at, you will need to track and review several numbers. A few will be your key performance indicators (KPIs) which are tracked and reported daily. The other numbers will be stored to be used later in the future, like when you need to tell the company history to a potential investor or when you need to make an infographic. If you think that it is going to be hard to do this, with today's technology, it is quite easy thanks to tools like Kissmetrics, Mixpanel, Geckoboard, Chartbeat, Totango, and many others. You should not allow your ability to track multiple metrics distract you. You will want to capture everything, but you should only focus on what is important.

Depending on what metric you choose for your OMTM, it will be important early on. However, when it comes later on in your startup process, your startup scales will force you to focus on several metrics at once, but you will have the resources and experience to do this without losing track of what you are doing with your OMTM. You should also remember, and it's important that you must, that you will have an entire team of people you can delegate metrics to. Operation teams can take care of uptime and latency while your call center will need to focus on hold time and things of that nature.

When it comes to picking your OMTM, you will have to run multiple controlled experiments and compare the results. Keep in mind that the One Metric That Matters will change over time. For example, if you are focused on getting users and hopefully turning them into customers, your OMTM will most likely be tied to the channels that are going to work best for you to convert those who sign up to use your service into someone who actually pays to use your service. Focusing on retention, you will have to look at churn while you experiment with features, prices, and improving customer support. Your OMTM will change depending on the stage you are currently focused on. Do not be surprised if your OMTM changes at the drop of a hat.

Reasons to Use OMTM

1. OMTM will answer some of the important questions you will have. During your startup, you will have to try and answer a million questions at once while juggling a variety of responsibilities. You should always locate the riskiest area of your business, and that will be where your most important question lies. Once you find the right question, you will then know the metric you should track so you can answer your question. That metric will become your OMTM.

2. OMTM will force you to draw a line in the sand, making sure that you have set clear goals. Once you've figured out your main problem, you will set goals which will be your way of defining success.

3. OMTM focuses on the entire company. The name Avinash Kaushik is commonly referred to as "data puking". Thanks to OMTM, you can help your entire company focus on one thing at a time. A few ways to do this is to post your OMTM on web dashboards, in emails, and on TV screens in your office.

4. OMTM inspires experimentation. At this stage of your startup, you should appreciate how important it is to experiment. You have to work through your cycle of build – measure – learn frequently and quickly. To be successful in that, you should always encourage your teams to experiment. In the equation, it will lead to some small fs (failures), but you will not be able to punish your teams for that because failures are going to lead you towards the solution and will help you avoid the big F (failures). Each person in your organization needs to be inspired and encouraged to experiment. As everyone rallies together focusing on the OMTM, you will be given the opportunity to experiment on your own, so that it can be improved.

Drawing a Line in the Sand

Knowing the metric to focus on is not going to be enough. For example, you want to get new customers every week. So this will be your metric that you focus on while you are running your experiments. Even though you have decided what you will focus on, you will now need to find the proper question. How many new customers do you want a week? Or more specifically, how many new customers per acquisition channel a week? The first thing you will do is pick a number, and this will be your target. You have to believe that you can reach this goal so you can have success. However, if you do not hit your target, you will have to go back and figure out what to do to reach the goal.

Picking a target number is going to be difficult. This is one of the places where most startups struggle the most. Many times, this number is avoided and skipped over. Unfortunately, this means that it is hard to figure out when an experiment has been finished. So, looking back to our new customer example, the experiment would fail because any number that had been picked would be immaterial. In other words, it is a failure. Should you become successful, then you will know based on the effort and time that you put into your experiments.

There are two right answers to the question of "what does success look like?" The first answer is that it will come from your business model which is going to tell you what a metric will be. So, if you need 10% of your users to sign up for your services where they have to pay for it, and that meets your target number, then that will be the number you will stick with.

In the beginning stages of your business, you will still be figuring out what your business model is going to look like. It will not tell you exactly what you need. Therefore, the second right answer is to locate the normal or ideal model. You should have an industry baseline, so you know what is most likely going to happen which will allow you to compare yourself to it. If you do not have this information, you will need to start here.

The Squeeze Toy

There is another part of OMTM that is important and the only way to understand it is to explain it as a squeeze toy.

By optimizing your business to maximize a single metric, you will be making something important happen. Just like a stress squeeze toy, you will be squeezing your business in one place which will cause it to bulge in another which is a good thing! Optimizing the OMTM will squeeze your set metric making it, so you get the most out of it; therefore, revealing the next place you will need to focus your efforts. This is going to usually happen at an inflection point of your business.

The Lean Enterprise Experiment Canvas

The success of Lean startup methodology can be seen in large enterprises such as Amazon and GE. This is because they have decided to implement some of the key principles of Lean Startups so that they can understand the difficulty of the markets they deal with and the disruptive innovation's speed.

Even though the Lean Enterprise canvas is self-explanatory, it is better to have a guide that can help you show your team how the canvas should be used.

1. *Clarify important metrics and draw your line in the sand.* As you know, your top priority will be the OMTM which you will need to use to track the changes that occur to your services and products that will eventually affect the goals of your business. For most startups, this will mean that you need to locate a product market fit as well as a business model. For larger companies, OMTM will differ based on the department. Customer service will focus on keeping customers and getting new customers, while IT will want to focus on how many items are delivered. After you've known what metric to concentrate on, the current value should be defined first before starting with the experiment. In the event that you do not know what the current value is, you need to figure it out. But what if you can't figure it out? Then you will have to develop the instrumentation to do it. Having the metric and its baseline in mind, you will need to start with a target value for that metric so you can manage all of your team's expectations. In other words, you will be drawing a line in the sand for your organization. As we've said, your target needs to be ambitious with high goals. Even if you do not reach your goal, a small achievement is better than not being able to reach a small goal. Celebrating any success is going to boost your team's morale, but you should not lose sight of all the work you still have to do. Even if you cannot reach your goal at all, you need to remember your line is in the sand and not in stone. You can always change it later!

It is recommended that you define a variable you can control and keep track of. When you experiment, you run into risks. That is why this is advised. This is also to make sure that you can improve at least one KPI at the cost of your business. For example, by getting rid of a complaint form, you will be getting rid of all the complaints that you've gotten before, but it is not going to improve your customer satisfaction.

2. *Identify and prioritize the problems you're experiencing, but do it from your customer's perspective.* After you begin analyzing what you are offering your client, you need to identify the problems that you are facing. The more complex your customers, several business units, and market segments are, the more problems you will have to face. So, it must be kept in mind that every problem has its own importance.

When the problem is understandable to the perspective of the customer, you will make it easier to share and clarify the issue with your other teams.

You should always support your observation with customer feedback, the pattern of data, and other anecdotal evidence before you conclude that your observation is indeed a problem. The problem will become a validated one once you found the observations that will support it.

So you don't have to waste development time, your team should put their efforts into problems that have high potential and are highly important to your customer. There will be a side effect beneficial to you when you prioritize your problems because you can present the importance of the problem which makes it easier to get buy-in from your stakeholders.

3. *Define your solutions.* Define any solution that can be done with cross-functional teams. Every employee needs to be able to provide their own insight without judgment. What they have to say may help you discover the reason for the existence of the problem and its appropriate solution. The CEO will be in charge of strategizing while customer service should tackle the important complaints. From there, developers will need to know how to solve problems from a technical point of view. This includes at least one function that has to do with defining the solution. It will limit the chances that your local problem will have a negative impact on the entire business.

It is vital to keep in mind that most solutions are going to be more incremental or of a more radical nature. Some of the low-risk incremental experiments will receive more support from the organization. This is one of the most common traps because experimenting with incremental solutions will help you climb towards a local optimum. By allowing the identification of a radical but effective solution, experiments for solutions to your problems will be mixed with iterative improvements and large leaps for your organization. The iterative improvements will help you to move up your mountain, and the leaps will help you locate the highest mountains.

4. *Figure out which testing method will allow you to maximize your learning while minimizing your resources.* A big part of preventing waste is in the attempt to minimize the waste that you use in finding a solution. For many startups, this can come easy because they move fast and break stuff.

However, on the other hand, large companies have to be more careful because they have more at stake such as their reputation. Whenever it comes to building an MVP as a testing method, you must keep in mind that the minimal version needs to solve the original problem.

On top of that, the test will only be useful if you can act on the results you get. There are times that will require creativity and care.

5. *Before running the test, you should define first the success.* When you look for more positive results of your test, the cognitive bias should be strong. Your success criteria must be defined up front, so you are not getting overly optimistic once you've run the test.

6. *Get out of the building.* Two purposes serve the experimentation of the enterprises and services. A business model that is sustainable is what the Startups typically look for while experimenting to locate where the product fits in the market. Enterprises will already have a set of customers that are there for them so they can execute a scalable business model.

For enterprises, the goal is to get out of the building and find what is going to provide more value for their existing customers. There are many ways that this can be done such as:

1. Usability research

2. Customer interviews

3. Focus groups

4. Analytics

5. NPS surveys

7. *Results Analysis and see if the needle has moved.* This is vital and cannot be skipped! You should take note if the needle moved once the test has been run. You will have three choices based on the results you get:

- Declare success and implement the solution

- Pivot and try to find a solution to another problem

- Persevere and move on to the next column trying again.

It would be wonderful if all tests proved to offer some kind of success but that is not the real world, and there are going to be tests that are invalid. This is not bad, but you can save a lot of time if you have implemented a more validated solution. If you find that is an invalidated solution, you can locate another solution or focus on another problem.

Penny Machine

There is a story about an entrepreneur who walked into a boardroom and looked around at the table of investors before reaching into a leather bag. After pulling out a machine that was about two feet high, he set it on the table and plugged it in. Everyone stared at him as he asked them if they had a penny. One of the junior staff hands over a penny, and the entrepreneur tells them to walk.

After inserting the coin into the machine, he pulled a lever, and there was a whirring noise before a nickel fell out at the bottom of the machine. After this event has taken place, everyone is silent except for the air conditioner.

Finally, one of the older investors says that that was a neat trick and challenged him to do it again. Getting another coin, he does it again, and another nickel falls out. At this point, he is accused of having a bag of nickels in the machine and told to open the machine.

Without a word, he opened the machine and showed a series of tubes and wires but no space big enough to conceal nickels.

Curious now, the investor asks how many pennies an hour can be put into the machine. The entrepreneur says that it takes five seconds for the machine to cool down so 720 pennies can be put in it an hour which means that $36 in nickels are spat out, so there is a profit of $28.08 an hour!

Another partner sat back and looked around the room before asking if he could put nickels into it. The inventor says he put dimes into it, and dollar bills were spat back out, but nothing else had been tried, so he was hoping that it could handle fives. After that, he was asked how many could be made to run at once, and he answers.

The last question was why no one else could produce the machine, and it was because he was the only one who could produce legal currency thanks to an agreement he had with the US Mint.

While this isn't a real pitch, it is almost perfect. Much can be learned from this example, and it is often used for many startups, so that they can start thinking like investors instead of just as a CEO.

The penny machine is a chance for those to make money. By putting money in, money spits out. People are often familiar with what a penny is, but CEOs often become obsessed with making as much money as possible, and they lose track of where they started.

Another way to look at it is that the entrepreneur was excited to share his invention that helped hack the business model which made it to where he could hack the product.

If you look at the example, you see that one of the investors wants to know how big the business can grow, how good the margins are, and what kind of barriers it has upon entry.

The entrepreneur told his story only because the investors helped by asking the right questions. He was anticipating their questions and only giving enough detail to keep them asking more questions.

There is no need for detailed explanations at this part of the startup because right now, he is just trying to get the investors interested. But, later on, the investors will want to look at the technology to make sure it isn't a trick, immoral, or illegal. The very first message is about making sure that the machine is explained to everyone in the room on a level that they can understand regarding what they are investing in. The entrepreneur did not set any value to his invention. However, he still gave the investors the details that they needed so that they could form one of their own based on cost, margin, and revenue potential.

The startup CEOs are going to be seeking venture capital, but they need to keep in mind the penny machine. Each time your pitch starts to stray from making sure people understand what you are trying to sell them, it is a sign that you need to go back to what you are trying to sell and tighten it up. Do not stray!

People to Talk to

Look at the world around you. What do you see? You see a world that is not inclined to physical interaction because we have technology at our fingertips and we can talk to people who are miles away. Because of this, we do not see the body language that happens between us and the person that we are talking to which can be a waste of everyone's time in the end.

This is not to say technology is bad; instead, you should use it as a tool for finding prospects so you can take your business further than those that came before you were able to.

Twitter

Twitter is one of the best goldmines out there. Twitter has an asymmetric nature where you can follow someone, but they do not have to follow you back while allowing people to interact without too many barriers between them. However, because of our nature, whenever we mention someone, they find out, and they can see what was said and who said it. As long as this privilege is not abused, it is a wonderful tool to use for finding people.

So, if you are building a product that is geared towards teachers and you want to talk to the teachers near you, all you need to do is get on Twitter and put in the keywords and your location in the advanced search on Twitter. Once you hit search, you will get a list of organizations and people who will be what you are looking for. As long as you are careful, you can reach out to these people. Do not spam them right away; start getting to know them first before you try and ask them to participate in your project.

LinkedIn

Another place that you will find what you are looking for is LinkedIn. On LinkedIn, you will find a large amount of demographic data as you do your searches. Unlike with Twitter, you do not have to connect to those that you find in your searches because you will have all of the information right there and you can connect to them in person. However, if you do have someone in common, you will find that it is going to be easier for you to connect to them on LinkedIn and get the information you need.

Facebook

You will run into more risk with Facebook because the relationship has to be reciprocated. However, you can get a sense of how big the market is by looking at search results; you may even find some groups you can join to do your research.

AdWords

Thanks to Google, you can now make target campaigns. So if you want to promote a survey or something similar to it, you will be able to with remarkable precision. The first thing you will do is to set up the AdWords campaign. There will be places that allow you to specify the location, language, and other information you need from your targets.

Now that you've done this, you will create your message. This is a great place for you to try out your different taglines and approaches. Even if you do not get clicks on something, it gives you important data that you need to look at. You should also try a variety of appeals to basic human emotions. Learn what people are going to click on and what keeps them around long enough to reach out to you.

Chapter 5: Lean Enterprise

Lean Enterprise is a production and management style that looks at all the working parts of an enterprise that does not necessarily add value to the final product. Lean Enterprise will focus on adding value and getting rid of waste and any non-essential processes. For the most part, a Lean Enterprise looks at the product and service from the point of view of the customer to determine what its value is before moving on to examine the process that is used to create this product. The purpose of reducing the products aspects is to add value to the product.

Lean Enterprise is usually referred to as Lean, but both of these terms came around in 1990, as explained earlier. Another way to look at Lean Enterprise is that it is the maximization of value for the customer while reducing waste in the production process. In the end, a Lean Enterprise is going to be about creating the most value for the consumers by using the least amount of resources. This goal is perfect for the delivery of value to the customer by perfecting the production and delivery process.

Principles

James Womack and Daniel T. Jones stated that Lean Enterprise could be characterized by five main principles.

1. *Value:* This will pertain to how the product or service you are offering your customer relates to their wants and needs.

2. *Value stream:* Understanding the life cycle of a product or service from start to finish.

3. *Flow:* If there is any part of the value stream that becomes stagnant, then it is considered waste, and it is not going to be providing any value to the customer.

4. *Pull:* The directive that nothing needs to be produced until it is demanded or ordered but the customer.

5. *Perfection:* All sub-par quality needs to be eliminated from the manufacturing process.

Lean Enterprise and Six Sigma

Lean Enterprise borrows eight different directives that are based on the Six Sigma principles. These principles help to get rid of waste from the beginning of the process to the end of it, and it is known as muda. The acronym 'downtime' is the best way to remember the word.

D – Defects

O – Overproduction

W – Waiting

N – Non-Utilized Talent

T – Transportation

I – Inventory

M – Motion

E – Extra processing

From Production to Enterprise

As you've noticed throughout this book, when a company embraces Lean production, they notice a dramatic improvement in their performances. As discussed earlier, this is done by eliminating unnecessary steps, aligning steps so that they flow properly, and reintegrating the labor to teams that are cross-functional, dedicated to one project at a time and strive for improvement constantly. Some companies can complete this process from start to finish with less or half of the human effort, space, expenses, time, and tools than they already do. They are also more flexible which makes them more responsive to customer desires.

Lean Enterprise is groups of functions, individuals, and companies that are legally separated but operate in sync. The Lean Enterprise is defined by the value stream. The Enterprise's mission is to focus and analyze the value stream so that they can supply a product or service in a way that can maximize the value to the customer. Lean Enterprise will differ from the virtual corporations where members are always going and coming. An entity that has no stability cannot sustain collaboration that is needed when applying Lean techniques along with the value stream.

When looking at the business structure of most companies today, there are not many that have not created a Lean Enterprise which is understandable. In doing this, there is a radical change in employment policies as well as the role of the functions inside the company which includes the relationship there is to the value stream. The focus of the managers will now be on how the company is performing instead of on the performance of employees or functions. This is vital because even though there will be a team leader, the enterprise is going to be brought together and share in each other's failures and victories.

Linking Lean activities can be difficult because managers are accustomed to overseeing a set of functions and narrowing down activities so that they can look out for their company's best interest. So why try out the Lean Enterprise when the others who have tried it are struggling to master its Lean production? They need to do this because, unless every member of the value stream is working together, a single person cannot maintain the needed momentum to keep the company running. That does not mean that a single person cannot make much advancement using this principle, but that member nor the entire stream will be able to reap the benefits in the event that someone does not do what they are supposed to do.

Three Needs

To have a successful value stream, it is vital to get managers to think in terms of the Lean Enterprise. Managers who take this first step typically face refusal from functional units and employees along as well as the other corporations in the stream. The three needs relate to individuals, functions, and companies that will occasionally have problems with the value stream. As long as everyone is aspiring towards the Lean Enterprise, they have to know how to satisfy these needs.

1. *Individual needs:* For many, a job is one of their minimum requirements for them. Therefore, it is ridiculous to conclude that people will orchestrate and identify the appropriate changes that could end up causing them to lose their jobs. Because using Lean can create a large number of extra workers, the need to constantly reduce the number of efforts and jobs can cause an obstacle when it comes to confronting an enterprise that is attempting to make a performance leap before they can sustain their momentum.

Outside of a job, most of us desire a career, so we have a sense of direction. On top of that, most of us need somewhere that we feel defined in our work lives. These needs can be fulfilled by telling people what we do and whom we do it for thanks to a company or a union. However, the value stream cannot fulfill these needs for that long. Even though companies usually stick around for a while, a company's position could be eliminated because of the value stream based on the way their position is tied to the products life.

2. *Needs of the function:* To expand and use the knowledge of the employees, the knowledge should be organized to functions wherein they can be useful. Functions will have more than accumulated knowledge which means they will help to teach that knowledge to those who identify their careers with that function. They are going to be constantly searching for new knowledge. In learning organizations, functions where learning is collected and then redeployed allow for functions to have a secure place in an organization. Since there is the knowledge that is required, time and effort needed to obtain this knowledge, and portability, it will make specialists feel stronger so that people can commit to their function and add value to the stream or the company. However, focusing on processes means that an organization has to be Lean and will require a high degree of

cross-functional cooperation. It should not surprise anyone that most executives view their own function as an obstacle.

Some business theorists and executives say that members of functions need to be assigned permanently to multifunctional teams as the solution to the conflict that happens between functions and processes. There are others that suggest weakening the functions such as marketing in a product team. Each solution will work for a short period of time, but it will end up causing problems in the end.

3. *The need of the company*: The company will find it easier to calculate the costs when they have a narrower scope of responsibility, so the benefits that it generates make it so that the results are the improvement efforts that the company was working towards.

Almost in the whole history of the industry, another company has taken over the others which aids in making up the chain or one company have integrated value chains to it vertically. An adequate return must be earned for the company to survive, making the practices more sensible. This also means that it will not be the end user market that will be the greater threat for the company to survive but the weak links in the chain. From this, companies will think that it is more important to have control than to have efficiency and responsiveness. During hard times, the biggest companies will naturally reincorporate as many activities it can handle inside the company. Every company in the value chain can also grab profits from the other companies during these hard times.

Hints

Because all of these needs conflict with each other, it is easy to understand why some companies attain flexibility, customer responsiveness, and maximum efficiency. However, this is only going to be helpful for a short spell before these needs start to cause issues once more.

As you try and find a solution, you should look at the three preeminent industrial traditions.

The German Tradition

The Germans' backbone always focused on the deep technical knowledge that was sorted into rigidly defined functions. Individuals can climb the functional ladder to advance their career more. And most companies hoard their knowledge about their technical functions to maintain their positions in the value chain.

The consequence of this function is that it has shown great technical depth and the ability for the Germans to compete across the globe thanks to their product's superior performance.

The American Tradition

In American society, the individual is at the center of it all. There is a lack of craft and strong functional traditions as well as the suppliers' willingness to collaborate with the variety of assemblers which brings in the majority of the advantages while presenting a mass production and constant flow.

On the other hand, needs are created by extreme individualism. In the era after the war, professional credentials are usually sought by managers while having generic expertise outside of their particular business. Instead of stressing cooperation, every company is out for itself.

The Japanese Tradition

The Japanese, not surprisingly, focus on the company's needs especially when you look at the Japanese feudal tradition between companies and their employees. Government policy focuses on production instead of the individual consumption which helps in reinforcing their emphasis. The biggest benefit is that big companies can focus on the needs of the value stream unimpeded by career paths or the constant struggle between members of the value stream trying to gain an advantage over others.

However, because of this exclusive focus, the company ends up producing weakness which has become more apparent over time.

Strategy for Lean Enterprises

Companies that join in a Lean Enterprise have to aim the opportunities that are great in order to exploit their competitive advantage. But this kind of thinking has to incorporate a new element so that it can sustain and complement new concepts that are in a Lean Enterprise. This element is: how can they find additional activities that can help to sustain the relationships that are based on their superior performance.

Because of its nature, Lean Enterprise will do more with fewer resources. This leap obviously requires the involvement of every person working for the company and all the allied companies. Every company in the value stream must work together to determine how much space they need, what kind of tools they need, the type of labor needed, how much labor is needed, and how much time they need to create their product. If an employee cannot create value, they must be returned to their home functions so that every member can focus on these activities. It cannot be implemented and sustained if there are extras that do not have a place.

To ensure that gains are not sustained as the productivity grows, the allies and employees may be dumped. Employees will have a need to save themselves over the value streams. On top of that, the public can become angry when a company fires several hundreds of people, which could end up causing the government to place restrictions on their ability to downsize.

Therefore, how do companies avoid mass layoffs? They lower prices which they pass on savings to their consumers, so the sales increase or they grab shares from competitors that were not able to implement Lean.

Obviously, not every company inside of an enterprise will be able to preserve all of the jobs. Some workers are laid off, and the supplies discarded by some companies in developed industries.

Companies explore all options for keeping these jobs while they create options to save jobs, but sometimes, layoffs are unavoidable which makes it easier for employees to accept.

The End Result

One effort that can be seen in companies across the industrial landscape is the embracing of Lean Enterprise and the organizations trying to locate new tasks for extra employees which will be superior to other industrial policies that the government comes up with. In an economy that is controlled by Lean Enterprise, they will constantly be doing their best to improve their flexibility, productivity, and responsiveness to their customers which could help to avoid social upheavals that occur whenever new production systems have been made obsolete.

Whenever things change in the industry, most people, companies, and enterprises prosper. It is also important that everyone witness the productivity explosion that is tied to employment stability that is going to be the solution that has been plaguing the advanced economies.

Chapter 6: Lean Manufacturing

The main idea of Lean manufacturing is that regardless of work, a company will want to get rid of waste from their manufacturing process.

But what qualifies as waste? Waste is defined as anything that does not add value to a product from the customer's perspective. According to the Lean Enterprise Research Centre (LERC), over 60% of production activities in a usual manufacturing operation qualify for waste because they are not adding value for the customer.

There is good news though! Every company has the chance to improve by implementing Lean manufacturing techniques and an assortment of other manufacturing best practices. These techniques will allow you to deliver a higher quality product for less.

TPM

TPM stands for total productive maintenance. You will need to get your operators involved in keeping up with their own equipment and place emphasis on proactive and preventative maintenance which will help to lay a foundation for improved production.

You will want to try and avoid breakdowns, slow running, or small stops in your machines, and no defects caused by your machine. When you are proactive with your machine, you are creating a safer working environment that means that there are not going to be accidents!

TPM is going to blur the lines between production and maintenance by helping operators become empowered to maintain their own equipment. By implementing a TPM program, there will be a shared responsibility for equipment that will encourage people to be more involved. When this is implemented in the right environment, it can improve productivity.

Traditional TPM

When looking at the traditional approach to TPM, you will discover that it was established in the 1960s and comprises of a foundation made of 5s with pillars, the eight supporting activities.

The 5s Foundation

The purpose of this is to develop a workplace environment that is well organized and safe for your employees which means you will need to implement five elements:

1. *Sustain:* make sure your standards are being applied.

2. *Sort:* get rid of anything that you do not need in your workspace.

3. *Standardize*: create standards for when you are performing your activities.

4. *Set out:* organize your items in your workspace, so you are not searching for them.

5. *Shine:* clean your area daily.

It should make sense how 5s creates the perfect foundation for making sure your equipment is running properly. For instance, when your area is well organized, and your tools are easy to find, you can easily see things that may have been hard to see before such as, spills, cracks, wear and tear, and leaks.

The Eight Pillars

The eight pillars will focus on being proactive and attempting to prevent any issues with the equipment.

1. *Autonomous maintenance:* You will be responsible for routine maintenance like inspection and cleaning in the hands of the operators.

a. The equipment can be owned more by the operator.

b. It frees up the maintenance personnel for the more important tasks.

c. It increases the operator's knowledge of the equipment they are using.

d. It identifies any major issues that may occur before they become failures.

e. It makes sure that the equipment is well cleaned and lubricated.

2. *Planned maintenance:* Maintenance will be scheduled based on any predicted failures or previous failures.

a. Reduces the inventory because you will have better control of the parts that are worn through faster or could fail first.

b. Reduces unplanned stop times.

c. Makes sure that most maintenance is planned when the equipment is not being used.

3. *Quality maintenance:* Create a system that can detect and prevent error in the production process by applying the root cause analysis so you can eliminate using sources of quality defects.

a. This will reduce the cost because you will catch defects early.

b. Targets quality issues by improving projects and focusing on getting rid of the defects' root sources.

c. Gets rid of how many defects occur.

4. *Focused improvement:* Those small groups of employees that proactively work together should be placed so you can achieve improvements in the operation of your equipment regularly.

a. By combining all the talents of the company, you can create a workplace that fosters continuous improvement.

b. Problems that keep reoccurring can be identified and resolved by the cross-functional teams.

5. *Early equipment management:* Takes understanding and practical knowledge of manufacturing equipment and directs it through the TPM by enhancing the equipment's design.

a. Maintenance is more robust and simple because of the employee involvement and practical reviews before it is installed.

b. New equipment must reach the planned performance levels faster because there will be fewer startup issues.

6. *Training and education:* If there are any knowledge gaps, they need to be filled so that TPM goals can be reached. This will apply to everyone from the operators to the managers.

a. Managers must be trained in TPM along with helping employees with coaching and development on TPM.

b. Operators will create the skills they need to identify any emerging problems and maintain the equipment.

c. Maintenance will learn techniques so they can be proactive and take preventative steps.

7. *Safety, Health, Environment:* Keeping the working environment safe and healthy.

a. Targets the goal of keeping the workplace accident-free.

b. Gets rid of any health and safety risks.

8. *TPM in administration:* TPM techniques can be applied in administrative functions to help further keep the workplace safe.

> a. Supporting production through improved administrative operations makes the workplace run smoother.

> b. TPM benefits will move past the work floor by addressing the waste that can be found in administrative positions.

OEE and the Six Losses

OEE stands for overall equipment effectiveness which is a metric that will help you to identify the percentage of the really productive time. OEE was established to help TPM which will be used to track the progress so that companies can achieve the production perfectly.

> 1. Most manufacturers that do not use any Lean program or TPM typically have a 40% OEE score.

> 2. Discrete manufacturers have a typical OEE score of 60%.

> 3. OEE scores of 85% are given to world-class manufacturers.

> 4. A score of 100% is only used for those that have perfect production.

OEE will have three underlying components that will map out each of the TPM goals that were set out earlier, and each one is going to be taken into account based on the type of productivity loss.

> 1. *Availability.* The TPM goal for this is that there are no stops. Availability will take into account the loss that will include all of the events that stop any production that is planned for any length of time. Some examples include stops that are unplanned and planned stops.

> 2. *Performance.* The TPM goal is that there are no small stops nor slow running machines. The performance component will account for performance loss, and that is going to include every factor that causes production to operate at less than optimal speed. So, the goal is not to have any slow cycles or small stops.

> 3. *Quality:* The TPM goal is to have no defects. Quality is going to take into account quality loss which will factor out all of the manufactured pieces that are not meeting the quality standards or any pieces that need to be reworked.

> 4. *OEE:* The TPM goal is to reach perfect production. OEE is going to take into account all the losses that production may experience. This will result in a measure of a truly productive manufacturing time. OEE is going to be tightly coupled with TPM so that no breakdowns happen and there are no defects nor are there any slow running machines. It is vital that the OEE be measured so that the productivity can be exposed and quantified so that improvements can be tracked.

> 5.

Benefits of Automated OEE

Learning how to calculate OEE manually is a great way to learn the benefits of OEE. You can do this by sitting down with a piece of paper and a pen or even with a spreadsheet. You will only need five pieces of data while calculating the OEE: the planned production time, the stop times, the ideal cycle times, the total count, and the good count. While performing manual calculations, you will be able to reinforce the underlying concepts which will provide a deeper understanding of OEE. However, there are a few strong benefits that you can benefit from when you move on to automated OEE data.

1. *Stop time:* Manually calculating unplanned stop times will usually fall in the range of 60 to 80%. But with automatic run and downtime detected, the accuracy can be moved up to 100%.

2. *Small stops and slow cycles:* For most equipment, you cannot track slow cycles and small stops manually. This means that much of the data you need to use for your measurements will be based on time and event-based loss patterns that are not going to be available.

3. *Operator focus:* Thanks to automated data collection, the machine operator can spend more time focusing on the equipment instead of focusing on paperwork.

4. *Real-time results:* Automated data collection will provide results in real time which means you can see your improvements faster, and in turn, you can start using improvement techniques like SIC (short interval control).

Creating the Best OEE Goal

You should think about how to set an effective stretch goal for your OEE. There are a few techniques that you can use known as the best of the best and here is how you will use these techniques:

1. You need to track your OEE for the equipment you want to improve for at least a month. You need to ensure that shifts compile all the results.

2. Review all the shift results. Make a note of the best results per shift.

3. Multiply your best results to calculate the best of the best. This new calculation will represent your stretch goal which has been derived from the best results that are achieved throughout the month.

Understanding the Big Losses

OEE loss categories can be explained further in terms of the Six Big Losses, which are the most common losses in productivity. These losses are important because they are universal in every application for discrete manufacturing. They will also provide a framework that will get you to start thinking about waste in your manufacturing process and how you can get rid of it.

1. *Unplanned stops:* The OEE category is availability loss. A few examples of unplanned stops are tooling failures, motor failures, and overheated bearings. Unplanned stops are flexible based on where the threshold is set between an unplanned stop and a small stop.

2. *Setup and adjustments:* The OEE category is availability loss. Examples include warm-up times, setup and changeovers, and operator shortages. The setup and adjustment loss will usually be addressed based on setup time reduction programs.

3. *Small stops:* This OEE category is a performance loss. Examples of a small stop include having to clean and check the machine, component jams or sensor jams. Most of these small stops will last less than five minutes and are not going to require maintenance personnel.

4. *Slow running:* Another performance loss. You can find slow running losses in equipment wear or incorrect settings. If it is going to keep the equipment from running at its maximum speed, it will fall under the slow running loss.

5. *Production defects:* This is a quality loss. It includes examples like scrapping and reworking your product. Any rejections that have to be done during the steady state of production will fall under this category.

6. *Reduced yield:* Another quality loss that can be found in scrapping and reworking product. You'll have to find these rejects during the early production stages.

A great way to understand TPM is to walk through an example where it is implemented. Here, we will walk through a short example for you to understand TPM better.

Step One: Identify the Pilot Area

Here, you will locate your target equipment for the pilot TPM program. There are three ways to pick which one you want to work on.

1. *The easiest to improve:* You will find a quick win with this piece of equipment, but you are not going to get much payback in improving the constraint of the equipment.

2. *Bottleneck:* Instantly increases output. You may find that the result in the equipment being offline is better so you can improve its output.

3. *Most problematic:* By improving this machine, you will be supported by the operators. However, you will find that unsolved problems are usually unsolved for a reason.

Step Two: Fix Your Equipment, so it is in Prime Working Condition

Your equipment will need to be cleaned up and prepped to be improved. You will be using your 5s and autonomous maintenance in this step. Both the operators and the maintenance personnel will need to follow the 5s program.

1. Take a picture of the initial state of the equipment.

2. Clean out all the debris and other components that are not needed.

3. Organize anything that is left in the workspace.

4. Clean the equipment and surrounding areas.

5. Take another picture of the improved state and post with the other picture.

6. Create a 5s checklist.

7. Schedule audits to verify the checklist is being followed.

You should put the machine on an autonomous maintenance program and build a consensus between maintenance and operators on what tasks need to be performed by the operators. Sometimes, a little bit of training is required, but usually, it can be done by the operator without issue.

Step Three: Measure OEE

There needs to be a system in place that can track the OEE of the target equipment. This system can be manual, but the scope of the system has to include unplanned stop times. For most equipment, the biggest losses are there because of unplanned stop times. It is recommended that you categorize every unplanned stop to get a better picture of where you are losing production time. It is also recommended that you include a category for unallocated stop time.

Step Four: Address Major Losses

Here, you will need to look at the biggest sources as to why you are experiencing a loss of production time. TPM will help here when you look at the focused improvement pillar.

1. Select your losses based on the data that you have gathered.

2. Create a team to address the problem.

3. Collect more information about the symptoms and any observations you make.

4. Organize solutions for the problem.

5. Schedule a stop time to fix the issues.

6. Restart your production with the hopes that everything has been fixed.

Step Five: Introduce Proactive Techniques

In this step, you will implement proactive techniques for maintenance of your machines.

You will need to identify all the components that are going to need to fall under the proactive maintenance program. Things that are going to fail will be the worn parts because of use and the stress points of the machine.

Next, you need to figure out the proactive intervals for your maintenance. Look at your parts based on wear, on a specific time schedule, when you predict that it will fail, and when a work order has been placed on it.

Chapter 7: Scrum

Scrum is an innovative way of transforming the way that people work because it is a disciplined approach to smoothing out the process by getting rid of pressure and waste.

Scrum originated from the work that Hirotaka Takeuchi and Ikujiro Nonaka did when they watched teams at Honda, 3M, HP, and Fuji-Xerox exhibit behavior that was similar to how Rugby teams acted. These two grandfathers of Scrum decided to create a concept of knowledge by creating a company and describing how a product can emerge from the knowledge that is generated from the dynamic interaction of a team. Lean shows how knowledge can be used in that environment, but Scrum is based on a complex adaptive system that reflects the self-organization that was seen at Toyota by Nonaka, and which can be seen in many Lean companies. Scrum is going to affect Lean indirectly, but everything about Scrum can be explained thanks to the Lean concepts. Scrum implementations improve dramatically thanks to those who understand Lean.

Scrum and Lean will join together on an assortment of aspects, and it is always nice to see what Scrum shares with Lean. Scrum and Lean are going to inform each other of ways that they can better implement the other.

Pillars of Lean

It was Fujio Cho, the president of Toyota in the 90's, that changed the two pillars of Lean to continuous improvement and respect for people.

Respect For People

Respect means that teams must work together, and you have to remember that you are working with humans. As you can see in the Agile Manifesto, Scrum teams find that one of the biggest things that powers it is the individuals and interactions. People create the value for products and services, not the process used.

Toyota has a saying that goes "Life goes by second after second and every second is important." Scrum helps to show value on time while focusing on features that are considered valuable to the users which can be estimated by those doing the job and delivering the product.

From a Lean perspective, software that is built in an iterative, incremental way is similar to building small batches that focus on customer value. The sprints seen in Scrum are going to be short amounts of time (typically one to four weeks) where the team focuses on developing the software the works.

What you are going to get from a Lean point of view will be opportunities that you can use to learn and understand better what the customer needs. This is because the customer does not know what they want until they see it put before them. Scrum adopted a mantra from the Massachusetts Institute of Technology's (MIT's) Media Lab known as "Demo or die!" This means that there has to be a demo for the customer or else the product is going to die.

There are many ways that you can show respect for those in Scrum. This is the opposite of the waterfall model where there are not GANTT planning that lists what needs to be done. With Scrum, the best strategy is to get customers in the room, but if you cannot, then you need to find a product owner that can represent what the customer needs.

The product owner will help in being the proxy to what the customer needs and attempting to develop something that will help with the release. You want to try and keep your releases as short as possible so that you can respect human life.

When looking at the customer, it is better to see a product as fast as possible while it is being developed because it may not be what they had in mind before. Words are a bad way to communicate, so you will want to try and keep it visual. The developer needs to develop something that is of value for the customer and confirm that it brings value to the customer as fast as possible so that they are not wasting time if things go wrong. The shareholder will want to know, as fast as possible, that there is a market for the product so that they are not putting money into something that will cause them to lose money. Scrum can also be seen as a way to avoid wasting things. Lean helps to improve in a continuous way, especially when trying to eliminate waste. Therefore, Scrum and Lean both point in the same direction.

Teamwork

Scrum practice is built to help run a team. Teams are collections of people that are there to challenge the team members and help each person reach their fullest potential. People constantly work towards mastery so that they can be the best that they can be.

With Scrum, the leader will be known as the Scrum Master. The Scrum Master role is not going to be there to monitor or report for the team, but more to prepare them, so they operate at peak performance. To achieve that, the Scrum Master will help the team by reverting the command control hierarchical pyramid so that people can create value, and the management is there to help.

Scrum Masters will help to protect the team from any interruptions. So what does this mean from a Lean perspective?

The first will be the strategy deployment also known as hoshin kanri. After you've set up the sprint, you will not work on any other issue, and you will focus on things that will help achieve the objectives of the business. Once you have created an environment where people are expected to live up to their fullest potential, then they will feel the need to reach their goals.

This means that you have to make sure that on a day-to-day basis, you are doing the same things so that your process can be better understood and improve. In the event that the flow production is not smoothed out, then you will find that you are running crisis to crisis.

Hiding Mura

The companies that attempt to hide mura end up creating extra inventory. Whenever there is more inventory created, muda is created. To remove this muda, you have to work on the mura.

One of the most crippling examples is when software is created, but it is not tested. Then you will have an inventory that is unfinished. By finishing the work at a later date, it will cost you twice as much as it would have to test and fix the bust instantly. In fact, it could cost up to 24 times as much as the work cost you. Since testing is going to have a constraint on the delivery, deployment could end up being delayed up to 24 times.

Scrum Master Environment and Working on Muda

You should not assume the capacity in which your team is delivering. You will discover this in your first sprint. For example, you have a team that is delivering 20 points. You have to face it and assume that you can deliver 20 points for every sprint. After you find your speed, you will be able to level out your production to ensure you are not going too slow or too fast.

Keep in mind that the goal is to get a team that will deliver, learn, improve, and innovate. With Lean, that means you will use the leveling strategy to create a stable environment.

With Scrum, you will keep a log of the features that you want to use in the next sprint and the features that are most valued by customers as long as they correspond with the capacity of the team after you have estimated every feature with a planning poker all while ensuring that there is a buffer.

With Lean, there is a concept known as takt which is the tempo given by the customers on the production line after you have leveled to produce every item. For instance, you have 60 cars to produce in six hours, so you will attempt to produce ten cars every hour or one car every six minutes. The customer leveled their demand which set the tempo for the production rate. This will work for production because it is based on a product, however, when it comes to IT projects, how do you translate it?

Inside the projects that you need to produce according to the customer's needs, you will backlog and prioritize the features at a pace in which the sprint allows based on the employees' understanding and learning.

Within the release, you will have to deliver a product to your customer. You will have to do it as fast as your team can deliver it or not. It will take at least three sprints before you can learn more about what your team can do, and from there, you can adapt.

There are several ways that you can adapt. It is safe to assume that you can learn at a fast rate but that does not mean you will be able to deliver at the same rate in which you learn. One strategy you can use is to get help from more people. Another strategy is to improve your team's productivity so that more work can get done with the same amount of people. The second approach is going to be at the core of learning for your team. Right now, let's assume that the number of points you need for your release is compatible with your team's capacity and the time that you have available to you. If your release plan looks good, how can you make sure that you are keeping it on the right track?

A burndown chart will give you the number of points that have to be done by the end of your sprint. You can also read it as the number of points that need to be done by every milestone production.

So, if you need to produce 60 points in six days, you will need to produce at least ten points a day.

With takt, you are given the number of points that have to be done for each period of work. With your Scrum daily meeting, you will follow your production each day and make sure that the team knows where you land on your production points. This information will allow you to act on your information and improve where you need to.

Thanks to the board, you will be allowing features to be pulled instead of pushed, and this is your Kanban board that is working with the new features you enter after you have finished other features.

Scrum provides you with practices that allow your team to steer clear of muri and mura and these practices help your team to focus on what your customer thinks is important. This helps your team prevent things that are not valued.

Do Not Ship Your Junk

A Lean aspect is building quality in your product by never allowing your defects to get to the customer. So, how can we help make this happen?

Your team will need to see the defect as soon as possible so you can have a concept of "good". But what do you define as a good job? If your team understands what your definition of good is, then they will have the ability to clarify the criteria to make sure that your task is completed.

What This Means in Lean

To avoid bugs, you have to create a device that is mistake-proof such as a test harness. This is typically known as poka-yoke. One of the best things is that your mistake-proofing device will help you prevent mistakes, but it can also be used to create alerts if something goes wrong. This will be the role of test driven development where you will write your how-to demo as well as write your test code before you write your actual code. One of the most interesting things will be when you coach your team to think of how you can validate the quality of the job instead of the productivity. You will find that it is easy to write code, but that does not mean that it will be worth something.

Therefore, you will discover that it is harder to write a code that does not produce any bugs. So this means that the test has to be run in a continuous way which is where the continuous integration will take place. Continuous integration will test your code, automatically providing you with a warning if there is a bug. This helps your team work on the error quickly before more appear.

Scrum allows your team to learn faster and create better code. All of this will be based on the respect that you create with your team by not making them do work that they do not need to do. It also means that you do not allow them to be randomly disrupted by helping others to have respect for the customer which makes the world a better place to work.

One oversight that many westerners have while looking at Lean is "There is no kaizen without hansei". Hansei is a deep sense of regret, repentance, and shame for dysfunctional behavior channeled toward positive redirection. It is something that too often is lost in the translation from Japanese Lean into American Lean and through to Scrum.

From there, we can enter the other pillar of Lean that creates a competitive difference.

Continuous Improvement

The true difference with Lean is that it attempts to provide every person the capacity to do kaizen. In other words, it gives them the chance to improve continuously!

This redefines your job, so your formula is: job = work + kaizen

So this means that each person will have a responsibility to do their job but also to search how they can improve their task. There are only good opportunities for problems to be worked on because any problem in the system is going to create waste.

Creating a Good Environment

It is hard for people to realize that there is a problem not just in their company but also in their team or within themselves. The problem that we do not see can sometimes make us act or behave in a certain way. The important part of constantly improving so that we are allowed to change the way we think in a controlled environment is by using a scientific approach.

There is no way for you to convince people by simply talking to them. Instead, the only way to do it is to try a solution they think of and see if it changes the result. As humans, we learn by doing, and we change our actions to change the results.

Learning to Ride a Bike

You do not learn how to ride a bike by looking at a PowerPoint presentation. You learn by trying. You learn by getting up and trying again each time that you fall down.

Lean offers you a scientific approach so you can better understand problems and find the tools that you can use to fix the situation. If you stay focused on the tools and techniques, then you will not be able to get the results that you want in the end.

Lean is not all about processes, tools, or reviews. It is about people because only people can think of solutions to problems. Lean is about getting people to improve their job continually.

Using Constant Improvement in the Real World

The only way to keep improving is to try and apply it to every part of your job. So, the question is, what teaches kata?

Kata is made up of five questions:

1. What is your challenge?

2. What is the situation?

3. What is preventing you from reaching your goal?

4. What is your next step?

5. When can we see what we learned from the previous step?

One thing that you may find interesting about kata is that it is simple and positive while relying on the approach that was described by Dan Pink where people have to perform in an intellectual environment: autonomy, mastery, and goal.

Goal: What is Your Challenge?

Autonomy: You are part of a team where everyone is going to help each other to perform better.

Mastery: You understand what is expected of you and you can deliver it or you learn what you have to do to deliver it.

In Scrum, there is a technical debt which helps the code get bigger while the system becomes more complex. This causes the technical debt to increase. Therefore, you will see the velocity go down.

One of the first things that Lean will teach is to "stabilize first".

Lean: job = work + kaizen

Scrum: code = new features + continuous improvement on what already exists in order to create new.

Chapter 8: Agile Project Management

Agile is a method that uses sprints and short development cycles for project management. The main focus of sprints is the continuous improvement of a service or product.

Even though the incremental development method can be dated back to 1957, Agile was first talked about in the 70s in a paper written by William Royce that talks about the large software systems development. It was not until 2001 that 17 developers published the Agile Manifesto with four key values and 12 principles that were meant to help guide an approach centered on the people. These developers got together in order to discuss lightweight development methods that they combine based on their experience.

Principles of Agile

1. Customer satisfaction should be your top priority which can be achieved through continuous and rapid delivery.

2. As environments change, the various stages of the process will help to provide the clients with an advantage competitively.

3. Products or services have to be delivered with high frequency.

4. Developers and stakeholders collaborate daily.

5. Every stakeholder and team member will need to stay motivated for optimal project results. Each team will provide all of the proper tools and support, and all of them will be trusted to help reach the project's goals.

6. Meetings that are done face-to-face will be more efficient and will promote project success.

7. The final product has to be the ultimate measure of success.

8. Sustaining development is only going to be accomplished through an Agile process where all the stakeholders and development teams can maintain an ongoing pace.

9. Agility can be enhanced through a constant focus thanks to the proper design.

10. Simplicity is essential!

11. Teams that can organize themselves are going to be able to develop a better design and meet their requirements.

12. Regular intervals should be used by the teams so that they can improve their efficiency by fine-tuning their behaviors.

Methodology Adoption

Even though it was originally made for the software industry, most industries use Agile as they go through the development process for their products thanks to the more efficient and highly collaborative nature of the strategy. Below, you will see how the adoption rates for the Agile methodology vary in some industries.

1. software: 23%

2. financial: 14%

3. professional: 12%

4. insurance: 6%

5. healthcare: 6%

6. government: 5%

7. telecoms: 4%

8. transportation: 4%

9. manufacturing: 4%

Benefits of Agile

Agile was developed to streamline and improve processes so that issues can be quickly identified and adjusted. This provides developers and teams with a way to make sure their product is better and is delivered faster and in a shorter period of time. Thanks to digital transformations, most companies have begun to lean towards digital workplaces. Agile is still able to fit into this digital world because organizations are going to look to transform how projects are managed and operated. Agile helps to make sure that the processes used across the entire company and the methodology align together.

The business benefits of Agile include:

1. Increased flexibility

2. Increased stakeholder satisfaction and engagement

3. Increased productivity

4. A decrease of objects that may have been missed

5. Increased transparency

6. Higher quality of deliverables

Advantages of Agile for Management

Agile provides team projects and all those involved with a few project-specific benefits in project management:

1. An increase of collaboration and feedback

2. Rapid-deployment solutions

3. Increase in customer needs

4. Reduced waste through minimization of resources

5. Project control

6. Increased flexibility and ability to adaptation

7. Lighter framework

8. Increased success and focused efforts

9. Optimized development processes

10. Faster turnaround time

11. Faster detection of defects

Drawbacks

Just like any other methodology, Agile is not going to be suited for every project, and it is always best for you to find the best methodology for every situation. Agile will not work if the customer cannot be clear on their goals, if the team does not function under pressure, or if the manager or team is inexperienced. Agile will favor the project teams, the customer's goals, and the developers through the development process, but it will not necessarily meet the user's experience. Because Agile is more flexible but less formal, larger organizations cannot absorb it easily because there are rigid processes or teams. It may also face problems when you run into customers that have operating methods or rigid processes.

Combining Agile with Other Methodologies

The chance to mix Agile with other methodologies like waterfall will create a hybrid solution. These companies sometimes use waterfall to handle multiple phases like planning, where they do not require rapid or repeated steps. Planning usually requires a comprehensive method that is usually slower when it comes to defining, documenting, and analyzing the aspects of the project. This is why waterfall is a better approach. After a project enters its development phase, these changes will need a different approach which is where Agile will deliver the best results in the shortest amount of time.

This new hybrid helps make sure that Agile will suit the special nature of the product or project, or is more adaptable with several industries. Just keep in mind that due diligence is required!

Popular Methodologies

Agile has a few popular methods that it can be used with such as Scrum. Below are some popular methods that you can use Agile with:

1. RAD (Rapid Application Development)

2. Scrum

3. Scrumban

4. Kanban

5. Feature driven development (FDD)

6. Lean (LN)

7. Disciplined Agile Delivery

8. Dynamic System Development Model (DSDM)

9. Crystal Clear Methods

10. Extreme Programming (XP)

11. Agile Unified Process (AUP)

12. Crystal

13. Adaptive Software Development (ASD)

Scrum and Agile

Scrum is a framework wherein Agile processes are implemented with software development. This framework that is adopted will utilize short periods of working which are known as springs. There are also daily meetings that are meant to discuss, in succession, parts of the project, until the project has been completed.

There are a few roles in Scrum that are vital, and they are the Scrum team members, the product owner, and the Scrum Master:

1. The product's owner will create and prioritize the backlog.

2. The items picked from the backlog and the ways of completing the work must be formulated by the team. Work has to be completed inside of a sprint.

3. The team will give daily updates to the Scrum Master.

4. At the end of every sprint, the sprint reviews need to be conducted.

5. The process will again begin until every item on the log has been reviewed.

Organizational Hurdles

Many organizations want to adopt Agile, but there are some hurdles that they have to look at before they pick to use Agile:

1. *The company's structure does not support Agile:* The rest of the company may not be ready to accept Agile even though the teams need to be ready for Agile. Everyone has to buy into Agile for it to be effective.

2. *The impact of Agile on the goals of the business is not completely understood:* Just by doing projects with Agile is not enough to get the results that you want. Projects have to be executed in a way that does not provide the business with a result that helps them to achieve growth.

3. *Rushed testing:* Sprints may create risks for rushed testing. When trying to get through the sprint as quickly as possible, the teams can become focused on the timeline and miss aspects of the testing cycle which could end up having repercussions. This is when defects go undetected or are found too late.

4. *Limited Agile skill:* Even though Agile is taking root, top Agile talent is hard to find and even harder to attract. Limited Agile talent equals limited benefits for the company that wants to execute projects with Agile.

Key Skills

There are six key skills that the Agile project management managers need to have:

1. A high level of adaptability so that change can be accepted to reduce risk and confusion.

2. The capability to focus on what is important and get through unnecessary work.

3. The ability to think and make decisions based on circumstances that are constantly changing.

4. Sound judgment under pressure and the ability to stay calm.

5. Great organizational skills that keep everything prioritized.

6. Strong motivation skills to help guide and support teams through their projects.

Agile Certification and Training

The Agile methodology will pick up speed, and that means that professionals have to have knowledge of Agile and experience in it. Seven certifications provide a benchmark for Agile knowledge:

1. Scrum Alliance

2. PMI ACP

3. Scaled Agile Academy

4. APMG International

5. Agile Certification Institute

6. Strategy Certificate in Agile (Associate or Masters)

7. International Consortium for Agile (ICAgile)

Agile Software

The companies that use Agile are most likely going to use software that is aimed towards Agile development so that they can reap the full benefits of Agile. Some solutions are:

1. *Version one:* This solution is built to help support the scaled Agile framework on every level.

2. *Atlassian jira + Agile:* This tool will support Kanban, Scrum, and an assortment of other methodologies. This project software will come with a set of tools that assist Scrum teams in performing events with ease.

3. *Sprint ground:* This tool is geared toward developers so they can organize their work and track their progress.

4. *Agilean:* Agilean helps automate the workflow for smaller IT companies. It can be customized and has 50 templates built-in.

Tools and Other Resources

There are a lot of different templates available from companies such as Microsoft that allow project managers to recreate the wheel:

1. Use Agile in Microsoft project

2. Agile glossary

3. Scrum process work item types and flow

4. Agile process guides

5. Scrum process

6. Agile process item types and flow

7. Backlogs

The Agile software vendors usually have built-in Agile templates inside their software.

The Future

With competition constantly growing and the time to get into the market shrinking, Agile provides many benefits with very few drawbacks. While more companies shift towards a digital workplace, they have to be fast, flexible and be able to increase their productivity, which means that they need to use programs like Agile and hybrid methods. Agile can be seen in many industries, and it aligns with the benefits offered by digital workplace models which indicate that adoption rates will increase around the world.

Chapter 9: Kanban

"A regular cadence or, heartbeat, establishes the capability of a team to reliably deliver working software at a dependable velocity. An organization that delivers at a regular cadence has established its process capability and can easily measure its capacity." – Mary Poppendieck

One of the things that set Kanban apart from Scrum is that Kanban decouples its cadences. Cadences are regular rhythms of activity. For instance, every two weeks, a meeting is held. So, at the end of each sprint that you hold, there is a review meeting. After you fulfill a few of these, you will have created a cadence of consistent productivity.

Imagine that there are no cadences, but you still have to hold the meetings. Things will fall apart because all the meetings will become emergency-driven and no one is going to want to attend the meetings; therefore, productivity will not be as high as it could be.

So, why are there development meetings every two weeks? Why will a spring need to be reviewed at the end? When are cadences decoupled? This is because Kanban provides teams with permission to try different rules. Just like after every sprint or development meeting, the stakeholders will have the time to get together and discuss the progress that the project is making.

David Anderson wrote about seven Kanban cadences, but there has not been one described to where everyone can understand it. Here, you will learn what the cadences for Kanban are.

> 1. *Stand up meeting:* Stand up meetings are frequent meetings that serve to help keep everyone on the same page and keep up with the status of the project. It helps to address questions like "who is working on what?" and "who needs help?" This is done to provide the team with information that they need so that the best decisions can be made about how team members should be using their time efficiently. This is a space for feedback to be given to the team by the stakeholders so that they know how to help. Stand up meetings are typically short, and the format can change based on the round of Scrum you are currently on.

2. *Replenishment meeting:* This is a pull system that will need tasks in the input queue to avoid becoming starved. These meetings are planning meetings where you will decide what these tasks are going to be. Scrum calls this a sprint planning meeting. However, the format could differ, and there could be several shareholders that are involved.

One of the first documented examples of Kanban was when David Anderson decided that regular replenishment meetings helped the team when it came to the prioritizing of income work from several managers. Therefore, he decided that bi-weekly teleconferences should be held and these managers would prioritize the work together.

The point of replenishment meetings is so that you can be updated on the progress of the project. This is one of the last steps that land between infinite possibilities and the commitment point of the system. This meeting will take the newest information from feedback to market forces, determining what the most important tasks have been fed into the system. These meetings need to be done frequently and must be transparent because the stakeholders trust what they have been promised will be delivered. All that matters is that the proper people are allowed to make the best decisions based on the proper data. A replenishment meeting is going to look different depending on its context. It may happen daily or even yearly. No matter how often it happens, it is a space where the efficiency of feedback and the speed of the delivery will be discussed. It may even happen on an as-needed basis which may be triggered by a minimal task and limit in the input queue, instead of doing it on a regular schedule.

3. *Operations review:* Operations review is a high-level view of how teams are working together. At this point, you should know where the shortcoming of optimization is. One start team is not able to save an organization if there is a poor delivery pipeline. A lot of the systemic inefficiencies will usually occur in handoffs. In these meetings, managers will look at ways to improve the system. By using the input from other cadences, managers can locate how the company is performing as a whole. Is everyone happy? Are you making money? Where can you improve?

4. *Delivery planning meeting:* This kind of meeting will acknowledge what many cannot deliver directly to the customer. It is the meeting that smoothes out the handoffs between teams. The next stage is that the customer may not feel appreciated because they are finding piles of work on their doorstep randomly. They would most likely appreciate being involved in the decision of how they receive their product. The teams will need to review the output of these daily meetings and the data that is found. You should take into account that there will be risks that arise in risk assessment and daily stand-up while looking to see what has already been delivered and what will be delivered soon. With input from those who are taking the delivery, they will be allowed to decide what to deliver and when it needs to be delivered. They will decide if any handoff activity training is required to make sure that there is a smooth transfer between teams. Because of this meeting, there will be

tasks that are in progress that change priority or class of service. For instance, the participants want an item to progress to be delivered next Tuesday and think that it can be, that means that the item's class of service will change to indicate that it is a top priority and now has a deadline.

5. *Service delivery review:* How are you serving your clients? The delivery review will examine the Kanban system from the point of view of those who matter, the beneficiaries of the service. A team's efficiency will be wasted if the customer is not happy. The service delivery review will include the representatives of the end users or outputs that explore the satisfaction of the customer from every aspect of the process. By reviewing the latest batch of work, you should look at the scope, SLAs, quality, and other criteria for the customer. Is the customer happy with what they received? How frequently is it delivered? Is the customer content with what you are providing them? Whenever something goes wrong, is the customer happy with how you react to their concerns and the way you communicate with them?

6. *Risk review:* A risk review can happen at any level of the company and needs to happen at all levels. The purpose of the risk review is to assess how likely it is that what you are delivering will fail. By identifying the risks, you can take steps to mitigate these risks and improve the system which will increase trust and profitability. The most basic level of risk review is to look at past failures and try to rework what was missed while identifying the root cause and locating a solution, so it does not happen again. Most comprehensive risk planning will include speculation of what is going to happen based on what has happened in the past. Plus, it will include input from all levels.

7. *Strategy review:* Strategy reviews will examine what has changed on the market and question if your current operational goals are optimized and serving the emerging needs. Are you truly efficient? Are you working together? Are you doing the right thing? Do you do the right thing needed to change based on market conditions? Are you building something to help your customers now or something that needs to be updated? In this meeting, you should review the company's strategy and make sure that your processes are delivering the best value with the best goal. You should compare your delivery times to the current market trends. Are there places where you can adopt? Is there a mismatch between what you can do and what you are offering? At the end of this meeting, you may find that you have a new set of guidelines when it comes to evaluating the product ideas or KPIs, so they are better aligned with market expectations.

Now, you know that you will have to look at a few things that could stop you from scheduling your meetings. Let's look at two scheduling mechanisms that you must consider so you can keep your cadences going:

1. *Time-based:* A time-based cadence will happen on a regular occurrence. For example, your meeting can be daily, weekly, or bi-weekly. This is great for situations where there is a value in constant updates or for things that should be discussed but are not urgent.

2. *Event-driven:* It is not written in stone that your cadences have to happen regularly. There can be a link to an event that keeps your cadence going. For instance, risk reviews can be monthly but can also happen because of critical failures. Deliver reviews may be every other year but can trigger the failure to meet SLAs.

That is a ton of meetings! But David Anderson said that by creating these seven cadences, this is not a way to add seven meetings to your life. Instead, you should try and use these cadences to see how stuff is being done and see if there are any gaps in your work so that they can be fixed.

Kanban Cards

The Kanban cards have evolved from what they were originally created for, but they are used for everything that has been discussed in this book. In the Kanban manifestations, the card and boards are great visual tools to minimize waste and increase productivity.

What Are Kanban Cards?

Kanban comes from the Japanese word meaning visual and card. Taiichi Ohno created the Kanban card system in the 1950s in order to manage the flow of the parts in his factory.

Kanban cards are still used today. It first stuck in a Piggly Wiggly supermarket whenever Ohno discovered that the shelves were stocked with just enough products to meet the buyers' needs. Inventory was only replenished when the shelf became empty, and this gave him the idea to create Kanban cards to get rid of unneeded inventory.

Why Kanban Cards Are Effective

Thanks to Ohno's concept, the emotional and psychological aspects have to be kept in mind. This is why there are guardrails that help to guide action and clarify what can make the system more efficient as well as empowering those who are contributing to it. Kanban cards have proven effective over time and can be seen in the four basic principles and six general practices.

Basic Principles

These four principles help to change management principles and describe what and how you can manage while staying efficient:

1. What do you do now? With Kanban, you will not be dictating a specific process. Instead, it will be used to examine all processes so that radical changes are not made instantly.

2. Agree to follow the incremental changes. By its nature, Kanban supports small changes to the current system. Radical changes are highly discouraged because they are typically met with resistance.

3. Sticking to the current processes and roles, Kanban does not prohibit or mandate changes while recognizing that the present state of the organization has value. Kanban's incremental changes will create wider implementation support since the small changes are easier to deal with.

4. Encourage leadership to act on all levels. Let them all know that they are supported and that they can all come up with ideas. Management does not have to be the only ones to come up with the ideas!

Six General Practices

1. *Visualize your workflow.* Kanban cards will be particularly helpful here. After you have seen the work, the number of requests, and the time that it takes for you to deliver the requests, you will be able to take steps to manage them as a team. The cards will be set on a Kanban board so all the team members can follow the workflow.

2. *Limit your work in progress.* This is vital for Kanban. By limiting your work in progress, the team can focus on a set number of tasks and getting them to completion. This will shine a light on where work has been obstructed before it becomes critical.

3. *Manage your flow.* Based on the data that you collect in your cycle time as well as any other metric that has been agreed upon, you can use this information on the current Kanban board. Kanban helps visually track and manage your projects.

4. *Make policies explicit.* Kanban teams will work together to set out rules and workflows based on what they are working on before moving to the next item. There will be notes that manage the blocked work tasks which will help the team work towards improvement.

5. *Implement feedback loops.* Many Kanban teams attend daily meetings while looking at their board so they can discuss ways to improve their delivery and their processes while getting rid of waste.

6. *Collaborate for improvement and experiment.* Kanban systems shine lights on areas that need to be improved on. After they have been highlighted, these groups can solve the problem through experimentation. By using the principles and general practices, Kanban can be used in every area of business. To be successful, your team has to buy into the system. Everyone will need to handle their own task inside of the standards that are set out, and the rules will have to be followed before the task is handed over to someone else. On top of that, Kanban information has to be kept up-to-date and must be easily accessed by every team member. This is why it makes more sense to have everything online!

The Art and Science

There are two categories that your cards will fall in, physical or digital. It does not matter if you are working with physical cards or virtual ones, the steps will be similar even though they may be more elaborate depending on the team size and the project. You have to remember that you are documenting the steps in your process and trying to improve your existing process.

1. *Visualize your work*. Break down all the steps from step one to the very last step. You will create a column for every step. You will also need to write your tasks on a different card. If you find it easier to color code your work, then do so! After you've done a task, move it to the right and move on to the next card.

2. *Limit your work in progress*. Even at 100% capacity, you will not be getting much done. No matter if the project is basic or complex or how many people are on the team, there is a limited amount of work that can be done at once while still being efficient. It is recommended that there are limits on your columns where the work is being performed. The goal of a work in progress is that things run smoothly and waste is eliminated.

3. *Adapt and improve*. Improvement has to be based on what you measure from your project. By using the data, you can adjust your process.

How Many Cards Do You Need?

One thing that many people wonder is how many cards to they really need? In a push system, the material and ideas can be moved in order to stick to a schedule that may be forced downstream no matter if the other person is ready or not. Push is also going to cause congestion which will grow the more that enters the queue. But in a pull system, Kanban will encourage everyone to work together and get rid of overproduction, underproduction, waste, control inventory, and limit work in progress. This can be applied to software development and knowledge work. You will find that there are formulas you can apply in a production facility where inventory is monitored which can be helpful in deciding how many cards should be used.

Formula: $y = DT (1 + x) / C$

Y – how many cards you need

D – demand per unit of time

T – the lead time

C – the capacity

X – the safety factor

Teams will need to determine how many cards are needed to manage their process effectively. The number of cards will change depending on the project and how complex it is as well as how many team members there are. Kanban is about learning what works best for you which means that if you need a lot of cards, you will need to use them. You should not stick to a set number of cards just because you used that many on the past project. If it doesn't work for this project, then adjust and move on.

Types of Boards and Cardholders

Physical cards can be used to track the process. You have to have a way to display them. If you are alone on your project, or you are working with a small team, your team needs to see the process status. Cardholders are on Kanban boards and allow cards to be moved so that the work progress can be updated as needed.

There are a variety of ways to display your inventory:

1. *Kanban bin system:* In a two-bin or three-bin holder, you will usually be tracking inventory, items that have to be reordered or are on a production line. A worker will pull the task from the first bin, and once it is empty, they will return the card or the entire bin over. The worker will then move on to the next bin while the first bin is replenished. If you are using a third bin, then it will be kept at the supplier's location.

2. *Kanban cardholders and racks:* This is often used for material handle environments and is mounted on a wall to show the flow of the project. The cards will signal the demand or capacity. The board will use magnets, colored washers, or sticky notes. Every object will represent an item in the process.

3. *Kanban board:* These are usually bulletin boards or whiteboards. These boards will track three areas of the workflow (to do, doing, done). Many people prefer to work this way because it provides a visual for what is being done and what is coming next.

Conclusion

Thank you for making it through to the end of *Lean: The Ultimate Guide to Lean Startup, Lean Six Sigma, Lean Analytics, Lean Enterprise, Lean Manufacturing, Scrum, Agile Project Management, and Kanban*. This book should have been informative and provided you with all of the tools you need to achieve your goals whatever they may be.

The next step is to start implementing Lean into your corporation so that you can see changes in your business! It is not going to happen overnight, but using the proper tools and resources, you can change your company so that it increases productivity and eliminates waste.

As you have learned in this book, there are different aspects of Lean and you will need to find the one that works for you. Having those that are experienced in Lean on your teams will make implementing Lean easier for you and your employees.

It is vital to remember that you should never ask your employees to do something that you would not do yourself! So, if you are not willing to implement Lean in your organization, then you must be able to follow your own rules. Your employees are not going to respect you nor will your improvement be successful if you do not follow your own rules. Learn and understand the knowledge of Lean and its other methodologies and know how it can be implemented best. Train your employees if need be for the betterment of the company.

Finally, if you found this book useful in any way, a review on Amazon is always appreciated!

Thanks for your support!

Part 2: Lean Startup

How to Work Smarter and Not Harder While Innovating Faster and Satisfying Customers

Introduction

The following chapters will discuss how to use the Lean Startup methodology to streamline your business and increase your profit. Lean Startup is an idea that is only a few years old, but it has been making big changes in the way that the business world, especially startups, implements and grows their businesses. Think about what it would feel like to know for sure that your product will do well and make you a ton of profits before it even hits the shelves. Lean Startup can provide you with the methodology to make this happen.

This guidebook takes an in-depth look at Lean Startup and why it is an amazing tool for your business. From understanding the principles that come with Lean Startup to working through your product, from the conception of an idea to production of a finished product, you are going to find all the techniques and answers that you need to make Lean Startup work for you.

Whether you have a great idea you want to use in your business or you are preparing to start your company, you will want to eliminate as much uncertainty present in the market as you can. Make sure to pay close attention to the contents of this guidebook to learn more about what Lean Startup is all about.

Chapter 1: What Is Lean Startup?

Lean Startup is about building your business from the ground up, with emphasis on fine-tuning a number of different aspects to create as much value from the very beginning while considerably reducing the amount of waste that will be generated.

Essentially, Lean Startup involves trying to do as much as you can to avoid overproducing, and this can be quite difficult to nail with precision in the early stages. It aims to eliminate as much waste as possible from the company's workflow by ensuring that those wasteful processes never start to manifest in the first place.

Lean Startup is rather different from the traditional business plan in a few key ways. First and foremost, it has a different focus and different demands. The Lean Startup business plan focuses largely on making incremental changes to a product or company to best meet consumer demands. Meanwhile, the traditional business plan might place little to no emphasis on initial consumer demands. Instead, it often pushes out a fully developed product to the market and from there reacts based on the product's market performance.

If this seems wasteful at first glance, that's because it is. It takes an immense amount of capital to start pushing out market-competitive and fully developed products, market them as necessary, then attempt to gain some sort of meaningful market statement. It's because of this that startup companies tend to be a large money-sink and a major capital risk. Lean Startup specifically aims to reduce capital risk and resource waste to make the process of starting a company easier on your pocketbook.

The simple fact is that having a startup is incredibly difficult. Most of the time, as a startup, you *don't* have the capital power that would allow you to anchor your entire company's fate on the success of a single product. The Lean Startup methodology could help with that aspect by giving you a way to save money on your company's initial launch.

While Lean Startup can be difficult to implement at times, there's no denying that it can help you see results in your business' bottom-line. What Lean Startup has to offer is a scientific approach not only to build startups from the ground up but also to manage it. It will also help you develop products and services that are aligned with what potential and existing customers desire, and it will teach you how to do so faster than ever before.

Working with Lean Startup, you can learn how to steer your business, what turns to take and when to take them, how to maneuver the obstacle-strewn paths, and how to persevere and keep at it until your business has grown in as speedy a manner as possible. This is a great way for anyone to approach the development of a new product or even a business idea.

Most new startups start with an idea for a product or service that they think the consumer will like. Then, they spend months or years trying to perfect that product. What they typically *won't* do is to take the time to show the product, in any form, to their potential clients. As such, they have no input from the customer, and that can make it hard to know for sure whether the customer will even like it once it's on the market. They'd also have little input on whether there are changes that they can make along the way to ensure the product will meet customer expectations. The failure to take these steps often leads to the failure of the startup in general. After the product comes out and the customers express through their indifference that they are not impressed with it, there's little else that can be done to remedy the situation. Nearly everything could amount to waste regardless of how hard they worked on the idea.

Lean Startup can help you circumvent these issues. It can ensure that your product will do well in the market because it won't have you spending years just to put together a product, all the while hoping it would take off. With Lean Startup, you will actually include the customers' input in your considerations and work from there. You can make changes to improve the product as you go, listen to feedback regarding these changes, and repeat the process, all to ensure that the final product you come up with perfectly suits your customers' needs.

The Lean Startup process

The Lean Startup process is often used when one wishes to establish a brand-new company or when there is a new company that wishes to introduce a new product to the market. This methodology advocates the development of products that consumers already demonstrated a desire for. This allows the company to know that there is already a market for their product and that this market will be open to it when the product is launched.

Traditionally, companies would work hard on a product and then release it to the market. Startups may fail, and established companies may lose a lot of money if they introduced a product that doesn't have a ready market. It was always a gamble, and that made it hard for many companies to get into the business world.

However, with the Lean Startup method, this risk and uncertainty went away. You would work on a product and take in customer information and feedback to figure out if potential buyers would be receptive. You could also make changes to the product or follow new and different product development paths based on the information you received from the customers.

When you employ Lean Startup principles, a developer will be better able to gauge the consumer interest in the product and then determine some of the refinements that the product may need. This is a process known as validated learning, and it is remarkable for helping the company avoid unnecessary use of resources when creating a product.

One nice thing about working with Lean Startup is that if your idea is likely to fail when it reaches the market, it is going to do so very quickly and cheaply rather than costing you a lot of money along the way. In this method, you will find that experimentation and testing are way more valuable than detailed planning. It considers a five-year business plan that has been built around uncertainty as a waste of time, but listening to the reaction of the customers is very critical.

Instead of spending time relying on business plans, Lean Startups base their business model on a hypothesis that they can test out quickly. Data doesn't need to be completed before they proceed; there just needs to be a sufficient amount. When the company sees that the customer is not reacting to the product as they desired, the company will then be able to quickly adjust to help limit its losses and then return a new product that the customer wants. In this method, failure is going to be seen as the rule rather than the exception.

This method can work for established businesses who are looking to release a new product onto the market, but Lean Startup is usually reserved for brand-new companies who are trying to get onto the market and who want to make sure that their product is going to be successful. Entrepreneurs who decide to go with the Lean Startup method will follow this method to test their hypotheses by engaging with their potential partners, purchasers, and customers. They do this to gauge the reactions from these people about the product pricing, features, distribution, and customer acquisition.

Once entrepreneurs gain the necessary information, they will then take their product and make small iterations or adjustments. If there are major changes that need to be done, they need to consider doing a pivot to correct any of these concerns. This testing phase can entail making many changes, including changing the product or even the target customer to make things work out.

Let's look at an example of how this works. There's a healthy meal delivery service, and their goal is to target busy, single 20-somethings in urban areas. By going through the Lean Startup method and listening to their customers, they may find that their business idea is great, but they are targeting the wrong type of customers. Instead, they might find that a much better market to work with would be 30-something affluent mothers of newborns who live in the suburbs.

Once the company finds out that it is better to serve a different market, they may make some other changes to the products and services to better serve this area. They may change the time that they deliver foods and even change what foods it will deliver so that they can provide good nutrition for these new mothers. They could also add some options for meals for other children in the house or for spouses of these mothers.

If the company had stuck with their original plan and not done the testing that is needed in Lean Startup, they may not have seen the sales that they wanted. They may have gotten some sales, but it is likely that they would have picked out a market that doesn't have much potential or one that has too much competition, and they may have failed.

The Lean Startup methodology will first look to identify a problem that the company needs to solve. It is then going to work to develop a minimum viable product, also known as the smallest form of the product that allows the entrepreneurs to introduce it to the potential customer. This allows the company to get feedback so that they can make changes that will make the product work better for the customer.

This method is actually faster and less expensive than working on the final product for testing, and it reduces the risks that startups face because it is going to decrease their high failure rate. It can redefine a startup as an organization that is searching for a scalable business model, not one that has an existing business plan that it is determined to execute.

Of course, this method is not just limited to startups. Companies like Intuit, Qualcomm, and General Electric have all used the Lean Startup methodology. For example, GE used this method to help them come up with a new battery that cell phone companies were able to use in developing countries where access to electricity was unreliable.

You will find that the Lean Startup method is going to be able to differentiate itself from the traditional business models even when it comes to hiring. As a Lean Startup, you must make sure that you hire workers who are can learn, adapt, and work quickly. Traditional businesses, on the other hand, tend to hire workers based on experience and ability.

These startups are also going to rely on different metrics for their financial reporting. Instead of focusing on their income statements, cash flow statements, and balance sheets, they are going to focus more on their customer churn rate, the lifetime value of their customers, how viral they can make the product, and how much it would cost them to acquire their customers.

Getting rid of uncertainty

Not having a tailored management process can cause a lot of chaos in your business. With the help of the Lean Startup approach, you can create more order, even while still in the early stages. There are many great tools that you can use to constantly test your vision. Lean is not just about spending less money, although this is one of the benefits of the program. It also isn't about failing cheap or fast. Putting a proven methodology in the development of your product so that it will do well is what it's all about. It is meant to help you do what you should do as a startup: grow high and grow fast.

Working smarter

Just because you have a good idea for a startup business doesn't mean that the business will necessarily be successful. It is not going to be just about the service or the product that you want to create; it is also about building up a sustainable infrastructure around your services and products. With the Lean Startup method, by the time your service or product is ready for mass distribution, it should already have some established customers.

Rather than simply hoping that the product you are developing is a good one and spending a lot of time on it while hoping that it will all work out, the Lean Startup methodology allows you to know for sure whether your product will do well or not before it even hits the shelves.

Creating an MVP

The minimum viable product, or MVP, should be front and center in your mental conception of Lean Startup. This methodology revolves around the process of *building*, *learning*, *measuring*, and *repeating* until the product is done. The first step is to determine the problem that you need to solve and then develop an MVP to help start the process. You want to do this part as quickly as possible.

Once your MVP is developed, you can then turn your attention to fine-tuning the engine of your startup. This involves a lot of learning, measuring, and a few other actionable metrics, for you learn how to produce the perfect project. You are going to spend a lot of this time investigating, and the best way to do this is to use the Five Whys approach.

This method would have you ask questions to study and then resolve the problems that your product may have along the way. If it is done the right way, it is going to help you know if you are moving in the right direction. If it is not, then it is time to do a "pivot" or enact corrections and try something new.

Validated learning

In the manufacturing side of business, the production of top-quality goods is the yardstick used to measure progress. In a Lean Startup, the unit of progress is known as validated learning. This is a rigorous method that you can use to demonstrate progress, especially if you are embroiled in extreme uncertainty.

When an entrepreneur jumps aboard the method of validated learning, the rate of your development may end up shrinking quite a bit. If you put all your focus on coming up with the right product to build – one that customers are more likely to pay for – then you would have to wait for the product beta launch that could still be months away before shifting gears and steering the company to another direction. However, with Lean Startup, you can adapt your plans incrementally as you go rather than wait until most of the work is done before making major changes.

Validated learning is one of your best tools when it comes to working with the Lean Startup method. With data to back it up, it would tell you if you have a market for your product when you are ready to sell it. Many startups of the past have failed because they simply created a product, put it on the market, advertised, and then hoped that the product would do well. Sometimes this works, but often it will fail simply because they didn't take the time to learn the market or make a product that the customer wanted.

Validated learning allows you to work on one product, polishing it into the version that the customer wants. For some startups, this may seem like it will take more time. Why would you want to go through multiple tests for a product before you ever got to sell it? Doesn't this seem like it is going to take more work before you can achieve anything?

In reality, validated learning actually takes less time. Which one would you rather do? Spend time making small changes as you develop the product to arrive at the perfect one? Or would you rather put in the whole nine yards of hard work only to find that, after the product is released, you have to make major changes – perhaps even start all over – before you can make money? Working with Lean Startup actually means that you will spend less time on development while still coming up with a product that the customer will purchase.

Chapter 2: The Benefits of Lean Startup

You can expect many great benefits when you decide to start using the principles of Lean Startup. This is meant to help make your business run better and help you succeed with confidence rather than just hoping that things will turn out for you in the end. Below are just some of these benefits.

You will be closer to your customers

While you do have to fight off some of the competition, there are natural advantages that you can enjoy. The first one is that you have a more direct access route for gaining input from your customers. And as mentioned before, you will also have the ability to implement changes based on the input that you hear in a fast and efficient manner. This is something that a lot of big companies are missing out on, and many wish they could do. The following are some of the ways you could use this benefit to win a competitive edge:

- Make sure that all of your employees are exposed to your customers.
- Establish a loop for feedback. This feedback loop should happen between sales.
- Take the time to study any interactions that occur in customer service.
- Monitor the social interactions as well.
- If you can, get on the phone and spend some time talking with your customers. If you have the ability, take the time to meet these customers in person as well.
- Mine the analytics that you get online.
- Incorporate the data gathered straight into the products that you produce.
- Make the feedback that you get from the customer highly visible across the organization.

You can make changes easily

Big companies are not really known for being nimble and agile. Often, the bigger the company gets, the more it is going to depend on established processes and structures. There is going to be more bureaucracy to deal with inside the company, and the lines of communication between the different departments can become less direct. Even worse, meetings, one of the biggest killers of productivity ever invented, will start to take over. As a result, planning for anything can take these big companies years instead of a few months or less.

As a startup, especially when you are working with Lean Startup, you can pivot and react to the different opportunities that come up in the market all the time. In the time that it would take a larger business to set up a conference call or a meeting to discuss the change, you can already have the change implemented.

When you take a look at how quickly the markets are changing nearly on a daily basis, you might find that it is nice to be a company that can keep up with all of it. Some of the bigger companies tend to get left behind because they don't know how to listen to their customers to get results. However, as a Lean Startup, you can make quick changes that your customers are going to notice and appreciate right away. There are several ways for you to exploit this advantage to get ahead:

- Pick a market that is evolving or that has some needs or tastes that are dynamic.
- Pick out a market that holds long-term innovation potential.
- Work on building up your market before the bigger companies even know what hits them. Doing so can really help you build up a good customer base before all the competition comes in.
- Use innovative and new technologies as well as business model components.
- Make sure that you can quickly evolve all the different aspects of your business.
- Try to get your senior management out on the field as much as you can.

You can develop a good focus on your target market

Large companies can sometimes run into trouble when it comes to focusing. They often have to worry about increasing their scope to sustain their growth, and sometimes, they have to develop products aimed at many different segments of customers using many different distribution approaches. Even though these large businesses have more resources than your startup does, they also have to spread out these resources in many different areas.

You, on the other hand, can devote all the resources that you have to develop a sharp focus on one very specific segment of customers. This is a huge advantage. Not only can you develop a deep understanding of your customers, including their buying processes, needs, wants, and pain points, but you are also better able to be clear and concise when you do any messaging.

The simple steps you can take to exploit this advantage include the following:

- Find a niche that you want to market to and go after it.
- Make sure that everyone who works at your company goes after that niche as well.
- Reinforce the focus any chance you get. Make sure the focus is coming from the top down as well.
- Make sure the team you have stays as small as possible.

You can chase after some of the smaller opportunities

Large companies are more likely to go after large market opportunities. They don't want to waste time or resources by going after a small market, especially if that market has special needs. This means that these larger companies are letting a significant amount of opportunities pass through the cracks. As a smaller Lean Startup, you can pounce on these opportunities and claim them as your own.

The key here is to identify and then attack the demographics and markets that, though they look small now, are heading upwards and possess much potential for growth. In the beginning, it can paint you into a tiny corner, but you can get the chance to establish yourself and grow without having to fight the big competition. You can then choose to expand later on if it works for you.

While some of these smaller opportunities may seem like they are a waste of your time to pursue, they can be quite profitable. You can make a good amount of money each quarter if you find and appeal to these groups, especially if they are ones who are ignored or underserved by some of the bigger corporations.

Some of the things that you can do to exploit this advantage include the following:

- Try to find some markets that are too small for some of the bigger companies. Find the markets that are off their radar.
- Find out if there are any segments of customers that have special needs which the big companies are not addressing.
- Pinpoint a latent or small market that startups are just starting to attack.

You can innovate more quickly and effectively

Change is sometimes a challenge for a big organization or a system that is well-established to deal with. They sometimes aren't looking to embrace risk at all either. For these companies, not only can it be difficult to coordinate the changes and the new initiatives from a logistical point of view, but there can also be a lot of resistance from the management and the employees.

To make things worse, there is a tendency in these big companies that can go against them: for incumbents, problem-solving and creative thinking are often confined to making small iterations and tweaks to a process that already exists. They often get stuck with the mindset "this is the way we've always done it." This leads them to not want to make any big changes, nearly stripping them of the ability to react and make changes that suit their customers.

As a Lean Startup, you are not stuck with these limitations. In fact, the more disruptive and innovative you are when developing your solution or business, the harder it is going to be for some of the bigger companies to compete, catch up, or copy what you are doing. This can give you a really big edge in the market.

Some of the steps that you can take to really exploit this advantage over some of the big companies are as follows:

- Take risks and be bold when you get started.
- Build technology that your competitors would run into trouble with if they stick to their current platforms.
- Execute an approach that would be very hard or disruptive for some of the larger companies to replicate.
- Employ your individual employees and teams to test, iterate, and then adopt the innovative approaches that you want.

You can keep your sales and marketing costs low

Lean Startup allows you to work at high efficiency when it comes to making profits. The basic idea that you want to keep in mind here is that everything you do, from your customer service and pricing to your product, should be so compelling that you can convert your customers with very little expense for marketing.

Of course, you do not want to cut out your marketing and sales altogether. But while the big companies have to spend millions of dollars each year to bring in the customers and get them to stay, you can get it done for a very small budget price. Your goal is to remain as efficient as possible. This helps you keep your costs down so that you can keep more of your profits in your own hands – and even keep the costs that you share with the customers down. There are several steps that you can take to fully exploit this advantage:

- Take the time to focus on UX.
- When creating your product, make sure that you build social sharing features into it.
- Make your sign up or your purchase process as simple as possible. If these processes are difficult to do, your customer will get mad or just give up, and you will never make the profits.
- Find ways to constantly improve the product that you are selling. Try to incorporate customer feedback with the help of a rapid development cycle.
- Allow customers the use of free beta and trial versions of your product. When you are done with that, take the time to price your product competitively.
- Make sure that your sales and your marketing expenses are as low as you can get them. This will allow you to put more money into the points above instead of just trying to get a hold of the customers.

Many startups assume that there is no way they can beat out some of the big-name competitors in their market. They think that they may be able to get a few customers here and there and that if they are lucky, they will be able to find a small market and maybe do well. However, with Lean Startup, you will realize that there is a lot of potentials out there for you. You can make some good dents in the competition as long as you leverage your size and what you can do.

Chapter 3: The Principles of Lean Startup

The ideas of Lean Startup have made some big changes in today's business world. It is now a thing that most companies work with when they are ready to start a new venture. To get Lean Startup to work well for you, you must understand and implement the main principles that are involved with it. The following are some of its main principles.

Entrepreneurship is the management

Remember that your startup is a full institution, not just a product. A product is going to be the main idea that you use to make money. However, you are going to make only a small amount if you only sell one product and if you don't build a company or an institution that can help to push that product onto the market.

Since your startup is also an institution, it is going to require management. This management needs to be something different and new, a type that is geared towards handling the type of products that you plan to sell. You want to have not only yourself as part of the management but also other people who share your vision and who are on the same team.

Do not hire someone to run the business if they only want to make money. You want to go with someone who can showcase their entrepreneurship in the work that they do. You want them to help you constantly build up the products that you want to make. With Lean Startup, you need to be able to work with the customers and constantly improve the product to make it perfect rather than just.

Entrepreneurs are everywhere

Nowadays, working from a garage is no longer a requirement to be considered a proper startup. Conversely, you also don't need to have a big office with lots of employees to be a startup. You just need to have an idea that you are looking to sell to your customers and the right mindset to get started. In today's modern world, you can find these entrepreneurs almost everywhere. Some are going to work from their homes, some will bake goodies and sell them, and some will take it to a bigger scale and actually run a business. But to get Lean Startup to work well for you, you must first be an entrepreneur who is ready to sell your product to the world.

You can be an entrepreneur as well. You don't need a big office to start pursuing your dreams of being one. You just have to own up to the title and steadily work towards that dream if you ever want to be successful, and you can always turn to the methods described in this book and in other resources to help you out.

Validated learning

Startups don't exist just to make stuff and money or to serve customers. They also serve as a platform for entrepreneurs to learn how to build a business that is sustainable and will last for more than a few years.

Many people who get into business feel that there is no way to tell ahead of time whether or not their business will be successful in the long term. They assume that it is a matter of luck or that it will be entirely dependent on the market whether they see success well into the future.

However, there are scientific ways you could use to validate whether your business is sustainable. This learning can be validated by running experiments that will allow you to test each aspect of your vision.

Innovation accounting

To help you improve your entrepreneurial outcomes and to make sure that you, as the entrepreneur, are held accountable for your actions, we also have to learn how to focus on the boring stuff. This means that you will need to set up ways to measure progress, set up milestones to make sure you are on track, and even learn how to prioritize your work. In addition, you must learn how to do a specific type of accounting that works best for startups.

Accounting in your first few years of business will be different compared to what you can use once the business is established and turning a profit. You will have to spend money in those first few years coming up with the product, paying employees, getting the materials, and paying back anyone who loaned you money. Having the right kind of accounting system in place will make a big difference in how well your business will do.

Build, measure, learn

The fundamental activity of your startup is to turn all your ideas into a product, measure how your customers respond to the product that you created, and then learn whether you should pivot or persevere based on the responses that you get from your customers.

This is a feedback loop that all startups need to learn how to follow. This is one of the best ways to figure out whether you are going to create a product that your customers really want or not. You can do this throughout the development process and even when you are ready to design a new product to keep the business sustainable. Never stop going through the loop of build, measure, learn. If you do, you are going to end up alienating your customers and not getting the sales that you want.

Understanding the principles of Lean Startup can make a big difference in how well you can make this all work. When you add all of these parts together, you are going to see some amazing results, no matter what types of products you want to sell or what type of business you are starting.

Chapter 4: The Concepts of Lean Startup

To understand Lean Startup, it is important to cover the key concepts behind it. This chapter will break down some of those key concepts to give you a deeper sense of what Lean Startup is and what it hopes to accomplish.

Minimum viable product (MVP)

The MVA is what we call the pilot version of a product whose main purpose is to provide you with information. It does not call for a massive investment on your part. What this does is give you an idea of whether or not a market exists without having to waste your time or resources extensively.

This is the initial step to take during the first round of testing the product. You need to have something concrete to present to the customer. The idea itself is not going to work because you'll be hard-pressed to find a customer who'll be satisfied with hearing your idea without being able to hold a tangible product in their hands.

With the MVP, you will need to go through all your ideas and pick one to work on. If you have a lot of good ideas, remember that you can always come back to them later. For the moment, you'll need to devote your time and energy to just one. Choose a product that you think will do well in the market, one that is really going to impress your customers, preferably one that won't take too many rounds of testing before it can be completed.

Once you have that idea, it is time to make it into a prototype. Remember that you need to have some kind of physical product that you can put into the hands of the consumer. At this stage, it doesn't have to be perfect. You are going to test it here and get advice and recommendations on what you should do next to improve the product. You can then build up from there and come up with a better version, and if needed, you'll need to repeat the process until you get it completely right.

There are likely going to be several different iterations of your product before you can bring it to market, and this will be especially true if you really listen to what your customers are telling you. They are going to give you valuable insights into what they like and don't like.

When you are working with the Lean Startup methodology, remember that the goal is to know ahead of time how the product will do once it's out on the market. You aren't going to run into surprises or find yourself lacking in sales when the product hits the shelves because you already made the necessary adjustments. But before you can go through and do those steps, you need to first come up with the MVP and work from there with the aid of your customers.

Continuous deployment

Continuous deployment in web and software development refers to the idea that all codes for a product must perpetually be in the production stages rather than development stages. This allows you to constantly receive feedback on the new versions from users, as well as have bugs be found and reported far more rapidly.

Software is a great example. The world of technology is always changing. New software comes out; old operating systems get updates. It is important that the software you create can keep up with all the changing demands of this world.

With continuous deployment, you can make constant changes to the software that you develop. Keeping an open forum with your customers can help as well. If someone finds a bug in the system, if you need to do an update because of new viruses that are out, or if some other issues come up with the software, you can keep it in continuous deployment to ensure that it is easy for the necessary changes to be implemented.

But continuous deployment doesn't just happen with software programs. It can work with any kind of product that you want to try and create. You should always aim to keep your product in continuous deployment so that you can address any issue that comes up. It could be as simple as fixing a bug in a program or adding a new feature to make the product work better for your customers. When you keep your product in continuous deployment, it is much easier for you to make these changes without having to start all over.

When you are working on your product, refrain from declaring to yourself and others that it is finished. The product should never become static and resistant to change. Even when you have come up with a product that your customers really like, it doesn't mean that you can just give up and never work on it again. Keep in mind that customers like having new things, that you may saturate the market with the current product, and that the needs of your customers will change.

When you keep the product in continuous deployment, you make it so much easier to make changes when you need to. You can add new features, get rid of some of the things that you no longer want, and so much more. This is just a better way to look at your products so that you can more quickly adapt it to the changing requirements without having to worry about starting over from scratch.

Split testing

Make two different versions of a product then release them to the customers at the same time. By doing this, you can glean information from how your customers interact with the two separate and distinct versions of the product. This can help you get an idea of which the market prefers, as well as give you data based on the differences among the preference of various users.

This is a great way to hurry through the testing process a bit more. You can even release one version to one group of customers and the other version to an entirely different group. From here, you can continue to test and see which one performs better, and you can then move forward with it.

Remember that the two products need to be nearly the same, but with one small difference. You can do this during several different iterations, but don't release more than two at a time. This will ensure that you get the right results when you need them and can prevent you from getting too much conflicting information from the work as well.

Only work with split testing if you are certain it will provide you with the benefits you are looking for. If this kind of testing is applied properly, it can give you a lot of information about your product while getting the work done much faster than other methods. If you don't do this kind of testing properly, however, it could give you a lot of mixed messages that you might not be able to sort out and use.

If you decide to go with split testing, make sure you follow the procedures properly. This will ensure that you can get as much information out of it as possible. This can be a great tool to help you when you are working with the testing in Lean Startup, as it can allow you to read through the information and feedback you get from the customer.

Pivot

A pivot is a specific course of action that you lay out which can allow you to have an alternate hypothesis about what else you think your company and resources could be used for. It's essentially a separate case and a backup plan that you can switch to if your first course doesn't work out without having to abandon the resources already accumulated.

This is something you need to work on if you find that your customers are not enthusiastic about your product. They may have much criticism about what you are doing, and you may find that there is too much that needs changing. In that case, it would be more efficient if you simply go in a completely different direction or start over with a new idea. That is what a pivot is for.

This is all a part of the process of Lean Startup. You need to learn what the customer wants, and it sometimes happens that the customer doesn't want the product that you originally provided. It is much better to learn this during the testing phase where you can easily make changes rather than after you've already put in a lot of time, effort, and money.

As an entrepreneur, you must be willing to enact the needed changes during a pivot. Sometimes, you can get really attached to a product you designed or worked so hard on, but if you don't listen to what your customers are telling you, you may end up with a product that no one wants, and you can't make any money from. You must be willing to pivot when the information and feedback you get from your customers make it obvious that it is needed.

Kanban

Many Lean Startup companies utilize Kanban boards. Kanban boards are divided into three categories – to do, doing, and done. They allow you to easily keep track of what tasks need to be completed and what tasks have been completed, especially in a team environment.

This is a great way for you to tell if you are heading in the right direction with the product that you are creating. Kanban is a nontechnical method that anyone on your team can work on. No one will feel left out if he or she is not creative, not technical, or not something else. You must always keep this board up-to-date to get the most benefit out of it. If you stop putting things in, it is not going to be the resource that you need it to be.

Lean Startup is meant to be a methodology that you can use to help you take your ideas and make them successful while also reducing some of the uncertainty that comes with the market. However, this is only going to work if you understand some of the concepts essential to Lean Startup and if you can implement them into your new business properly. Make sure to imbibe the concepts presented above and reflect on how you can apply them to your product.

Chapter 5: The Lean Startup Process

Let's say you have decided that you'd really like to model your company in the Lean Startup manner. How exactly can you go about it? In this chapter, we're going to be outlining a number of different factors that are immensely important to the development of your startup.

Step 1: Cement your idea

There are two types of startup owners out there: people who want to act on an idea and people who want to own a business. You can guess for yourself which one tends to produce the most innovative results.

People who come to the market with a new and creative idea are most often the ones whose companies enjoy the greatest success. However, that is not to say that having a derivative idea is necessarily bad. In fact, there are a bunch of *safe* businesses that anyone can start, including pizza joints, coffee houses, or even software development companies, and these make products similar to those already on the market and sell them at a lower price.

So, in the battle between safety and innovation, you need to decide which route you want to take. The Lean Startup idea tends to apply equally well to either, so that's a nice point of security. The only other consideration you need to think about is what *kind* of idea you want to have.

If you opened this book with a firm idea in mind, then you've already cleared this step. However, if you haven't quite got a solid idea yet, you need to start working on developing one first thing. What are some niches near you that aren't yet filled? What are some niches that *are* filled but you still want to get in on? Remember, markets are healthy when they have competitors, and they're also healthy when they have innovators. Either way, you need to have some kind of initial business idea at the ready.

If you are uncertain about what kind of idea you want to work with, it may be time to sit down and brainstorm. One cannot work with Lean Startup if one doesn't at least have a few original ideas that can be worked on. This would be the time to get out a pen and some paper and write down every idea you may have. This step can also be helpful even when you already have some that are concrete because you'll be able to compare them better.

Once you have come up with ideas, it is time to establish which one you want to work on. You can only pick one idea for the moment. While you may have many great ideas, you do not want to lose focus or have your scope change because you are working on too many things at once. Pick just one out and stick with it. You can always come back and develop some of those other ideas later on.

Step 2: Define your idea

Once you have your initial idea, you need to start working on the things that are linked intrinsically to it. What is the scope of the company you want to start? How do you want to branch out and develop from here? What can you start doing to make a meaningful start to your company and potentially push everything forward?

Figure out a path for your company and clarify a vision both for the near future and the distant future. Define in no uncertain terms what it is you want to do and what you ultimately want to happen down the line. In the next section, we'll be discussing a few different tools that you can use to help your startup-planning process go more smoothly.

Step 3: Start experimenting

At this point, you want to start playing around with your business idea. Everything in business and life involves experimentation, and startups are no exception. In fact, one could see startups as just one massive experiment. During this phase, you need to be telling people your ideas, testing others' reactions, toying around with and changing your idea, as well as tweaking it in certain ways. Essentially, do whatever you can to make meaningful shifts to your ideas so that people will want it *more*.

The experimenting part is a great time when it comes to the product development process. Use the scientific method and come up with a hypothesis that will further guide you. If you remember your time in middle and high school, you should still retain an idea of how the scientific method works. You would come up with a hypothesis, try it out, and then determine if you need to try something a different way, if your results were confirmed, or if you need a new hypothesis.

This is the same thing that you will be doing when you use Lean Startup and start experimenting with the product you want to make. You can work on the prototype and make simple changes, and at this point, these could be anything you like. See what works and what doesn't work, then move on from there.

The experimenting stage is crucial. It is definitely not a phase you want to miss out on. The more often that you can experiment and get your product into the hands of your customer, the better. This allows you to get a constant stream of information and feedback from your potential customers, and that information can be used to improve the product and make it better before you bring the product to market.

The experimenting stage doesn't have to be complicated; it just needs to lead you into making the right decisions as you develop your new product. Think about this as if you're getting ready for a science experiment or a science fair at school. You didn't just go out and immediately arrive at the finished project. If you did, you would have no idea how the final outcome happened and wouldn't be able to explain to the teacher, or anyone else, how it worked.

Instead, you looked at some of the problems that were going on around you. You picked one that you thought was the most interesting or the most pressing and decided to work on that. Looking at the information that you already know or could easily gather at the time, you formed a hypothesis or an educated guess about what would happen in your experiment.

Once the hypothesis was formed, you then moved on to experimenting. You would try out your hypothesis and see if you were right. Sometimes, you would have the right answer right from the start, but often, you needed to take a few attempts to get it right.

If you got a wrong answer, you didn't just give up. Instead, you looked to see if there were other ways to prove your hypothesis. After trying a few times, you may start to notice that some patterns are showing up, and perhaps from that, you figured out how to continue. Maybe you learned that your original hypothesis is wrong and that you needed to replace it.

Finally, you end the experiment with the perfect hypothesis and the results of your experiment prove that hypothesis to be true. You do well at the science fair, impress your teacher, and then move on with the day.

This same kind of idea can be used with your business process. You will start out with a hypothesis, something like "I think that the customer would like product A." You then develop product A, and when it is in its most basic form, you find a few potential customers who are willing to try it out for you.

After that initial review from the customers, you learn a few things. Some customers liked the product just the way it was. Since it is in the beginning stages, it's likely that most of the other customers would give suggestions on what to add, how to improve, and what things they didn't like about the product.

This doesn't mean that it's a "failed experiment"; it simply means that you have a few more steps to take before you are done. After that first review, you go back and take some of the suggestions into consideration, changing the product to implement some of the suggestions you gathered. When the changes are done, you present the product back to the potential customers (try to get a mix of them: some from the first time, some new), and then repeat the cycle over and over again until you get a product the customer loves.

In some instances, you will just go through and make some minor adjustments with each review of the product. Other times, you may get a few reviews in and find that your customers are not fond of the product at all. You may even decide to scrap your original idea and go with another idea that emerged during this time.

When you reach the end of this process, you will have a market-ready product or service, one that you know will do well with your customers. This process can take some time and energy, and you may even end up with a product that is completely different from what you first started out with. In the end, however, it helps to reduce some of the risks and ensures that you produce a product that will sell.

Step 4: Take risks

Understand that when you're working on an idea or a company, you're inherently taking a risk. There is no business without risk. Unfortunately, with startups, that usually means a loan or some sort of initial capital – generally saved up if not loaned out to you. You have to be willing to risk this now.

Every single startup has been, to one degree or another, a gamble – those who try to innovate present even bigger risks than those who aim to just fit neatly into existing market paradigms. To make your business take off, you need some initial capital, and if it can't come from your own pocket, you have to get a hold of it somehow. Procuring this capital through a loan is a risk in and of itself. This part of the process comes down to your willingness to put yourself out there, all to make your business a success.

If you are not ready to take risks, it may be time to take a step back and decide if this is really something that you want to do. The Lean Startup model is there to help you make smart decisions with your company, and it can definitely take away some of the risk factors. However, there will still be some risk that you must take on.

For example, while developing and creating your idea for a product or service, you will incur some costs: the product won't build itself for free. You will then provide it to the customer to hear their feedback and decide if you need to make any changes at all. In some cases, you may need just to tweak a few little things before you submit the product for some more testing. Other times, you may need to scrap your idea completely and start all over.

When the second thing happens, this results in wasted time and money. This can be disappointing for some new business owners, especially if they had decided that they were using Lean Startup to completely reduce their risks. Don't let the fear of losing a little money and time scare you away from this process though. Sure, you may have to spend some upfront costs, but the Lean Startup method ensures that you will make sales with your product because you know exactly what the customer wants.

While it can be scary to think of losing money long before you sell a product, think of how much better it is. Would you rather lose out on money in the beginning stages while you are developing your product or would you rather lose a bunch of money later on when you bring the product to market, and no one wants to purchase it? Take the risk early on and see how rewarding Lean Startup can be for you.

Step 5: Test your idea

This is one of the most critical parts of the entire process of Lean Startup. As we discussed in the previous chapter, the Lean Startup is about starting with really small basic products and then adjusting and incrementing your design as time goes on. It's from there that we springboard toward meaningful changes in your product that are specifically and absolutely tailored toward what customers want.

You can start this whole process by finding a test group and then asking them what they like and dislike about your product. This is considered reactive work, and it allows you to get a good idea of the market performance of your product while in actual use while also allowing you to eschew the high development costs and potential risks of putting a final product outright on the mass market.

In the chapter to follow, we'll be discussing a few tools you can use to actively receive real feedback on your products from people who are actually using them. This will put you in the driver's seat of your product's experience on the market instead of being forced to ride passively. This would also allow you to make worthwhile changes to your product based on actual use cases by real people.

There are a few different ways to test your product, but the most common are free trials or open beta programs. Testing is an important step that you have to follow as you work on your product. Companies who do not test their product ahead of time often see very lackluster sales. This is because they didn't include the customers in the process at all. They made an assumption that their product would be something that the customer would be interested in, but they weren't, and the product fell flat.

You will most likely go through several different variations of testing as you go about improving your product. Remember that when you test, it is best just to change one thing at a time during each iteration. If you start changing two or more things at a time, the messages that you get can get lost and confused. You may not know which feature the customer likes and which one they would want to be changed, and your product might fail as a result.

There may be some cases, however, when you need to do a complete pivot to make your customer happy. This means that you would have to change the idea you are working on or change the path that you are following to please the customer. This is perfectly normal. While it may be hard for new entrepreneurs to discard all their hard work, if the customer doesn't seem to like your product or company the way that it is, it would be a bad idea to keep going in the same direction.

The testing phase is going to be very important to your business. We discussed it a little bit in the sections above, but this is pretty much the way that Lean Startup ensures that your product is a hit with the customer and that you will actually be able to make money.

Many startups fail, and this usually happens because they work on a product and release it without having any idea how the public will react. With Lean Startup, you will focus a lot of attention on testing because this brings the customer into the process and can ensure that you have a product people actually want to buy.

What this means for you is that you should never shy away from testing out your product. Do as many tests as you can and actually listen to the information that the customer is giving you. This makes it easier for you to learn and it helps you make the right changes to improve your product and increase your chances of doing well as a startup.

Step 6: Measure your outcomes

This falls in line with the last concept. You have to measure what people are actually telling you. If you've released a piece of software, for example, learn from what they say they want in the program or where they say it falls short. If it's a prototype of a physical good, listen to what they think should be changed.

You can standardize this in one way or another by entering all of the responses into a spreadsheet and then sorting them by keyword based on what their concern is. This will give you a solid idea of which things are desired by most people. You can then incrementally approach and implement this.

You can get the information you need to measure the outcomes from the tests that you perform. After you have made a change to the product and given it to a test group of customers, you can then take a look at the reviews that they left behind. This is valuable information that you must use.

Following their advice is the best way to ensure that you create a product that customers will actually want. You could go along the traditional way and make products and hope that they do well on the market or you can use the methodology of Lean Startup and measure your outcomes from your testing to know for certain that the product is going to do well when you are done with it.

Step 7: Work adaptively

You need to work on your product and your company in such a way such that you can pivot around and make meaningful differences without changing your overall vision. For example, what if a lot of your user testing comes back and it turns out nobody wants the product you're making? On the one hand, you're lucky you found that out before applying it en masse only to face a massive debt and commercial failure. This actually puts you in a good position because on the other hand, while rejection stinks, it gives you the opportunity to change your idea and tweak your approach.

This is one of the benefits of being a small startup. You don't have a lot of overhead, departments, or money invested in what you do. When you see that there is a change in the market and you need to adapt, you can easily do it. As was stated before, this is an advantage over the bigger companies that you are in competition with. Make sure that you are always listening to your customers – even a tiny little fix or change to one of your products could be enough to help you provide better satisfaction.

Step 8: Work lightly

Be sure that you're only producing small amounts of your products at a time. This again is where you'll need to listen to your customers and take your cues from them. If you are working with a small niche market, then you probably don't need to produce a million units. You will only sell a small fraction of that, and the rest will be wasted energy, time, and money. Only produce the amount that you need, at the time that you need it.

This is a mistake that many businesses make, whether they are big or small. They get excited about their product. They want to be able to sell as much as possible and make a big profit. They may assume that there is a huge market out there for their product so why not just get as many items of it out there as possible right from the start? They may even be able to manufacture the large amount at a big discount, and they jump at that thought to increase their profits.

The problem here is that you are not really listening to your customer. You may be excited to get your product out there, and you may feel that everyone is going to fall in love with it and want one of their own, but this is not always going to happen. You never want to produce more than the amount your customers are likely to buy. If you do this, you will end up losing out on profits.

Before you go crazy with producing way too much of your product, think of it this way. How much money will you waste in producing the product, storing all the extra, moving the product (both the stuff that sells and the stuff that doesn't), and so on? These costs can add up quickly.

In Lean Startup, you need to learn how to produce only a small amount of the product that your customers demand. This can help you save money and not waste it on superfluous products that no one wants to purchase. If you run out of stock, simply produce more of the product. This is more efficient, especially when it comes to waste.

Step 9: Work innovatively

A successful company either fills a niche or innovates enough that their product or method can deprecate the old ones. Make sure that your startup, from the get-go, has an air of innovation and progressive development about it. It is through this air of innovation, as well as by making consistently solid products, that you're going to stay on top of the market.

Lean Startup is a great methodology that you can use to produce great new products that your customers will actually want to purchase – not products that will just end up sitting on the shelves. However, you have to make sure that you follow the steps properly. If you do, you are sure to see amazing results in terms of sales and the amount of customer satisfaction you receive.

Chapter 6: Lean Startup Tools

In this chapter, we're going to be covering a few different tools that you can use to help organize your Lean Startup.

Lean Canvas

In the last chapter, we made clear how important it is to really organize your thoughts on your business and come up with a solid business model. Lean Canvas allows you to make a simple and easy one-page business model that's equal in worth to twenty pages of a standard business plan. You can make as many as you want and share them with as many people as you need to. This is an indispensable tool for hopeful entrepreneurs. It's essentially an adaptation of the business model canvas, which is a popular template used to help businesses easily describe themselves and figure out their plan in their early formative stages.

Google Apps

This one might seem obvious, but Google Apps have a number of different tools built right into it that allow you to easily and effectively gather user data on their overall experience. These can also help you organize things for your Lean Startup from within. Don't be afraid to get started with Google Apps; you'll be glad you did.

User Testing

User Testing is a self-explanatory website where you can have real users try out your product. It will help you generate revenue as well as get instant insight into whether or not your product is highly usable. This is aimed more at internet startups, but it has a wide variety of different use cases.

While this is not going to be a replacement for face-to-face usability tests – and you should not consider using it in this manner – it is still a good tool to use in the early stages of development to help you pinpoint any usability issues with your product. The network of testers on this site can help you test anything that you want, including flat designs, a web app that you want to launch, or a stage prototype.

The testers on this site are there to help review your product, and they are going to provide you with some audio commentary while they do the work. You can hear what they think about the product, what they don't like, and some advice that they can give before the product goes live.

Bear in mind, though, that you don't get to choose the people who will review the item. The feedback will be from people who happen to be available to do the testing during a set duration of time. This means that while the testers can give you valuable insight, the results might not always give an exact or even a close indication of what your target audience is thinking about. However, for getting quick feedback to see if you are going in the right direction, Usertesting.com is a great option.

Proto.io

If you're planning to build an app for mobile users, you can prototype the service you'll be rolling out to users without writing any code at all and without spending a penny or time for the app's development. This site will provide a prototype that works on mobile devices and that you can actually have your users demo and respond to.

Upwork

Sometimes, you need to outsource work. If you find yourself in that sort of situation, you'd be smart to use Upwork. Upwork will help you find a bunch of freelancers to whom you can easily outsource the development of your site, your copy, or anything else to – without paying the price tag of a regular salary.

Intercom

The Intercom app allows your whole team to keep up with all of the users of your product. It gives you numerous different channels for keeping up with them, such as through e-mail and social media. This allows you to keep your test groups up-to-date on iterations and important changes, as well as to keep up with your users after you finally release the product.

Personapp

This is a good tool to use when you are trying to figure out if some changes are going to be good for your product. You need to work with actual potential customers as well, but this can help when you are trying to make a few decisions or are in the early steps before you get a chance to work with any other customers.

With Personapp, you can create quick and informal user personas that think like the people you are designing for. After trying some of the other options, Personapp is going to make things easier. You can choose to create a variety of personas for each project and then export this information for sharing and for printing. It can be immensely helpful, but you must first understand who your customer is to make this work properly.

Kiss Insights

Many Lean Startup companies want to be able to hear what their customers need so they can make sure that they are happy all the time. However, talking to each individual customer is difficult, if not outright impossible. Kiss Insights provides your customers with an easy-to-use method to let you know what they want and need. You can simply ask them a few questions, and your customers can see these come from the bottom right-hand corner of the site. You can even add a little spot for them to give some feedback. The customer will have a choice on whether or not to answer these questions, but the ones that do can provide you with valuable information about your products. Make sure to keep the questionnaire short and sweet. Two or three questions at the most are enough, or the customer will never follow through and answer your questions.

WuFoo

As you are working on your website, there may be times when you need to create some forms. This could be a contact form if your customer needs to get a hold of you, or it could be an order form or something else. Traditionally, you would need to hire a developer to do this, but with WuFoo, you can do the work all by yourself.

WoFoo makes it easy for you to create forms that you can embed to your site. You may want to use it as a way to get e-mail signups or to see if there is any interest in one of your product ideas before you go ahead and build it. It also has an interface that is very user-friendly so you can easily manage the forms that you create while also keeping track of conversions and analytics along the way.

Olark

If you are looking for a way to include a live chat so that you can better serve your customers, Olark is the company to work with. They are going to make it easier for you to reach your customers via your website. It will provide you with a simple and unobtrusive live chat widget that the customer can click on at any time.

Balsamiq Mockups

This is a good tool to use if you want to come up with wireframes that are interactive. The program is pretty easy to use, and even those who wouldn't consider themselves creatives are going to find that this program is really simple to pick out.

This is the software to go with if you need to find a way to visualize your product ideas without needing lots of documentation along the way. You won't need to create a technical spec. Instead, you can work with a low-fi Balsamiq wireframe and get the work done just as well.

KISSmetrics

This is a type of analytical software that you can use with your customers. From the first click to the last conversion, this tool can make it easy for you to identify, analyze, and then optimize the user experience throughout the entire customer life cycle. It is easy to work with, and it can ensure that you will fully understand what your customer is experiencing when they go through and work with your product.

Silverback

This is a great piece of software that can allow you to watch what the customer is doing when they interact online with your product, and it can help you see exactly what they are thinking at each stage. Silverback lets you record your live usability tests with the help of a built-in webcam and mic, and you can watch or share these tests whenever you need the information.

Along with helping you record the tester, it is also going to record all the screen activity that goes on while the user is testing out the product. This can help you know what is going on at each stage of the test. Being able to refer back to it later can be helpful if you need to write a report about the usability test sessions. You can also distribute these to others in the company to keep everyone on the same page.

Chapter 7: The Methods to Use with Lean Startup

The ideas of Lean Startup have truly changed the way that companies do business. Its methods are valuable whether you are a large established organization or a startup, which is also to say that it is valuable no matter what kind of product you are selling or how big or small your business is. This chapter is going to take a close look at how the Lean Startup methodology can help you innovate as well as create more value for your customer.

Build, measure, learn

If there had ever been an idea that, more than any other, succeeded in changing the way innovation is pursued today, it is the idea of bringing the scientific method in to help handle any uncertainties that arise in business. As covered before, using the scientific method means you need to define your hypothesis; choose a product or feature, build it on a small scale, and use that for testing the hypothesis; and learn continually from the results.

This seems like a simple method to use, but it has shown a ton of great results. And the best part is, it can enable a company to gamble on more than one idea at once because the risks are far smaller. The findings will allow them to determine which ideas they want to move forward with and which to discard. It is a much better option than putting all the bets on one product or idea only to see it fail.

This method is easily applicable to almost anything relating to business, not just to the new products you are designing. You can use it to: test a customer service idea, test out a review process with management, test out the text on your website, see the offers that you are giving your customers, and ascertain whether a new feature on a product that's already on the market is a good idea.

The important part here is that you can test and validate the hypothesis that you want to form. This means that you need to have the resources necessary to gather the amount of data or metrics and measure the results. With this method, the aim is to discover the most efficient way to cycle through the build, measure, and learn process. You will know at once whether it will be worth your time to go through another cycle or if you should stop and proceed with another one of your ideas. This means that you need to have an idea that is very specific before you test it and have a minimum number of items to measure. When it comes to a product, you want to test whether or not your customers actually want or need it.

Minimal viable product

Traditional product development is going to involve a ton of upfront work to explain the product's specifications clearly, and this is also going to include a significant amount of time and money that you must be willing to invest. The Lean Startup encourages you to build up only the most basic version of the product that you need to go through a single cycle of the build, measure, learn loop.

The good news is that you don't need to write lines of code to get an MVP. It could be something as simple as a slideshow that describes the journey of the customer or a set of mockups of the design. It is enough that you can test the hypothesis that you come up with using your real customers and manage to get enough validation and information so that you can go through another cycle of learning.

Vanity metrics

One of the basic requirements when working on a Lean Startup is having the correct knowledge and understanding of the process when testing a hypothesis. You will find that your business will easily start to focus on vanity metrics. These are metrics that can give you the feeling that you are making some progress with your work when, in reality, they are not really telling you anything of value about your product.

There are many vanity metrics out there, and they basically exist to make a business feel good. Listening to and basing your business decisions on them will make it hard for you to sustain and bring your business to the future. One example of a vanity metric is the number of likes that you get on Facebook.

While you are listening to customer information about your product or their reviews and feedback, it is crucial that you watch out for these vanity metrics. These types of metrics are designed to make you feel good and can often lead you to think that you are making a difference. Unfortunately, these are often wrong and will either give you no information or false information that leads you down the wrong path.

As a growing business, it is your responsibility to determine which metrics are the best for your needs. There are many metrics, but only certain ones will work well for your business type. Before you pick out the right metrics for your needs, it's important to understand some of the vanity metrics and what they are:

- *Views on your page*: This refers to how many pages on your website are clicked on during a specific amount of time. This can include a week, a month, a year, or more. Often, this is a waste to work with unless you are in a business that depends on page views, such as advertising. It is better to work with unique visitors to the site each month to help you make decisions.

- *How many visitors*: Yes, it can be helpful to know if anyone is visiting your website. You can then figure out if your website is easy to find or if it is as engaging as you wanted. However, often the information in this number is going to be too broad. For example, when we talk about the metric for "how many visitors", are we talking about one person who really loves this website and visits it fifty times or are we talking about fifty people who come to the site once? Your business most likely wants the latter scenario to be true because it means that you made more impressions, which can lead to more sales.

- *Number of followers, friends, and likes*: Social media sites are taking over the business world, and it seems like you can't succeed without having accounts on as many of them as possible. But you need to be careful about this vanity metric. This metric is going to give you a false sense of popularity, and it doesn't really tell you any information about the customer. A better metric to choose is the level of influence that you have over your followers. How many people will do what you want them to do? Yes, likes and followers on social media are nice, and there is nothing wrong with someone liking your information, but it is best to focus your attention on other metrics.

- *Email addresses*: Creating an email list is a great idea for a business. However, you must make sure that your list is full of useful and high-quality email addresses. It doesn't do you any good to have a list with thousands of people if most of them never respond to your information. It's much better to have a small email list with a lot of active followers who will be more likely to make a purchase from you.

- *How much time someone is on your website*: If you work in a business that gets paid for the amount of time someone is engaged on a website, then this metric is a great one to follow. For most companies, this metric doesn't tell them much about the customer. Sure, the customer may spend a lot of time on the website, but what if they spent most of it lost and frustrated that they couldn't find the information they wanted? What if they spent it writing a long customer complaint?

These metrics may seem like they are a great way to help you figure out what your customers want and to learn their buying behaviors, but they often just lead you down a dead-end road. Consider following more important metrics so that you can actually learn something from your customers.

The pivot

You will find that deciding to pivot on your project can be one of the hardest aspects of the Lean Startup method. This is because many entrepreneurs and founders are tied to their products emotionally, and the money and energy that they've put into their initial products are huge.

Problems like vanity metrics and not testing the right kinds of hypotheses can find your teams heading down the road of failure. An unclear hypothesis might make you feel that failure is unlikely because you simply don't know beyond the shadow of a doubt if the endeavor isn't working. A thought like "launch it and see what happens" is always going to give you a positive outcome because being able to see what happens when it does is the one certainty in this matter, but keep in mind that what you see might not be the thing that you want.

It is important to remember that the necessity to do a pivot does not equate to failure. It just means that you need to grit your teeth and abandon the fundamental hypothesis that you may have started out with in favor of something else that might work better. The pivot also comes in variations that include the following:

- *Zoom-in pivot*: This is when a single feature of your new product is turned into the entire product.
- *Zoom-out pivot*: This is the opposite of the above. This is when the whole product that you started out with will start to become a single feature in something that is much larger.
- *Customer segment pivot*: The product is just fine, but the original segment of the customers isn't. You may need to change the customer base that you advertise to, but the product itself will stay the same.
- *Customer need pivot*: This is when, through validated learning, it becomes clear that you need to work on solving a more important problem for the customer rather than working on the original.
- *Platform pivot*: Often, the platform that you have will start out as an application. Then it goes through a lot of popularity and has a lot of success, so it will grow out and start to become a platform ecosystem.
- *Business architecture pivot*: This is where you switch from an idea with high margin and low volume over to one with low margin and high volume.
- *Value capture pivot*: How the value is captured fundamentally changes everything else that is going on in your business. This can include some things like the product, the cost structure, and the marketing strategy.
- *Engine of growth pivot*: Startups are typically going to follow one of the paid, sticky, or viral growth models. To rev your growth quicker, changing from one of these models over to the other might be necessary.
- *Channel pivot*: With the internet as evolved as it is now, many more options and channels for startups have been created, and the complex advertising and sales channels are not as dominant as before. A startup has the benefit of using more options right from the beginning.
- *Technology pivot*: A new technology can offer you substantial benefits in performance, efficiency, or cost, and it can allow you to keep everything else the same. This includes keeping channels, customer segment, and value creation the same.

Just because you find that it is time to pivot doesn't mean that something went wrong with your product. It could mean that a minor idea that you had incorporated into your product is going to do better than the original one. It could mean that a competitor beat you to the idea and is already marketing it. It could also mean that the market is looking for something different and that you're in the best position to provide that to them.

Instead of looking at this pivot as a sign of failure, consider looking at it as a sign of a new opportunity or a new challenge. Sure, the original idea might not be working out the way you want, but think about all the other things that you could work on, the cool and unique products that you are going to release to the public now that you have reached your pivot point. Take all the information that your customers provided during your tests and use it to come up with something that is completely new and original. A pivot is a great way to make your product and idea much better than it was before.

Small Batches

Small batches can best be explained through a story. There was a man who had to insert newsletters into envelopes, and he recruited two of his kids to help him do it. The kids started off by suggesting a process wherein they fold all the newsletters as the first step, place stamps on the back of each envelope as the next step, and then finish by writing the address. Basically, they planned to do each distinct task one at a time and not alternate among the three. However, the man wanted to do it differently. His idea was to complete every envelope before moving on to the next one. They competed to see which method was the fastest.

The dad's method was the one that came on top because he had used the approach known as a single-piece flow, which is often employed in Lean manufacturing. Working on the same task repeatedly seems more efficient because there's an assumption that our speed and accuracy will improve as we do the same thing over and over again. But the individual performance is not going to be as important as the performance of the system as a whole. There is going to be time that is lost between the batches when you first need to restack all the letters then prepare all the envelopes. When you consider the three separate steps as one single batch, you can improve your efficiency.

Another benefit of working in small batches is that you can recognize an issue upon seeing one. Going back to the previous illustration, if you choose to complete each distinct task in one go only to find, after folding all of the letters, that they didn't fit inside the envelopes, you will have wasted your time and effort and would need to start all over again. However, if you worked in a small batch, you could catch your error right from the beginning and could then correct it before having to do all that work.

The small batch idea may seem a little counterintuitive to many people. We think that we can get things done so much faster if we do all of one large task first, and then the second, and then the third, and on until we are done, but this can actually slow us down. We have to double-check things, we make more mistakes, and we end up with a big mess and a tired mind and body before we even get one task completely done.

Think of how you would feel if you were working on the envelopes above. You worked hard and folded all of the papers just so, and then you try to put the first one in the envelope and found out it didn't fit. Since you folded all the papers the same way, you are now stuck with all these papers that won't fit inside their envelopes. You must now go back through everything and fix each one. If you did small batches, you would have realized right away that the paper didn't fit in the envelope. You would only have needed to re-adjust one thing and then make sure you did it the right way for the next batch.

The Andon Cord

The Andon Cord is a unique part of the Lean Startup that you can easily implement in your company. The Andon Cord was first used in the Toyota Company. It allowed any employee on the production line to call a stop to the system if they discovered a defect. Toyota found that the longer the defect continues along the production, the costlier it becomes and the harder it will be to remove.

When they were able to spot a problem right away, even if it meant that they needed to stop the whole production line to address it, they became more efficient. This is one of the main reasons that Toyota has such high levels of quality in their products.

The key to this Andon Cord is that it is going to bring work to a stop as soon as a quality problem surfaces, and the problem would be investigated. This is one of the biggest discoveries of the Lean manufacturing movement. It goes under the idea that you can't trade quality for time.

Kanban

We touched on Kanban earlier in the book, and here, we reiterate and explain further.

Kanban has four states:

- *Backlog*: These are items that are ready to be tackled but have not been taken up yet.
- *In progress*: These are items that are currently under development.
- *Built*: These are finished projects that are ready to be tested by your customer.
- *Validated*: This is the item's status when it has been released to the public after being positively validated by the customer.

A good practice is to make it so that each stage will only have three projects maximum at a time. If you have built a project, you won't be able to move it over to the validated stage until you've made sure there is room there. Thus, if there are already three in the validated stage, the other project will have to wait longer in the preceding stage. In addition, you can't start work on a backlog item until all the in-progress buckets have been freed up.

The Five Whys

Most of the technical problems that you will run into when working with Lean Startup will have a human cause at the root. Working with a technique known as Five Whys, you will easily be able to get closer to the root of that cause. It is a simple process, but it's very powerful in that it can ensure you'll figure out what went wrong and how you can fix it.

The Five Whys are illustrated as follows:

> 1. Your company released a new product feature, and it ended up disabling another feature. Why? Because one of your servers failed.
> 2. But why did that server end up failing? Because there was an obscure subsystem that your employees didn't use in the proper manner.
> 3. Why was this subsystem not used in the proper manner? The engineer who was put in charge of it and who uses it on a regular basis doesn't really know how to use it properly.
> 4. Why didn't the engineer know how to use it properly? Because he didn't receive the right education or training for it.
> 5. Why wasn't the engineer trained properly? Because your manager didn't have the time or the patience to train a new engineer.

You could go through this process and do it as many times as you need until you get down to the root cause of whatever issue is at hand. This is a great technique that many startups employ because it allows them to find the optimal speed to make the needed improvements.

When you take the time to look at the root causes of your problems, you will be better at identifying whether there are important areas that need your urgent attention. This can save you from always focusing only on the surface issues, especially since it is easy to overreact to things while they are happening. The Five Whys will make it simpler for you to take a deeper look at the issue at hand. Working with the Five Whys, you'll be able to root out the bad process, not people. It is a great way to get to the heart of the problem and solve it without having to point fingers at employees.

Working with the Five Whys, you can find what the root cause of your problem is. It is often tempting to go with the first problem that you run into, but this often leads to you missing out on the more critical cause that needs urgent attention. In the example above, if you just went to the third step and found that the subsystem wasn't used properly, you would probably blame the engineer for not knowing how to use the subsystem. This could result in some disciplinary action against the engineer and would most likely result in some low employee morale because they are not being given a fair chance. However, if you went further down the chain, you would see that the reason the engineer didn't know how to run the subsystem is that one of the upper managers didn't take the time to train the new engineer. You would need to either make sure your managers are training new employees the proper way or assist them in getting more help in that department because they might be overworked.

The Five Whys is there to help you find the cause that is really to blame, and often, the answers are going to surprise you. You shouldn't just stop asking questions after you've found one probable cause. Keep going through until there aren't any more Whys for you to ask. Doing so will lead you to the solution that can actually help the problem.

Some of the good practices that you should implement when you start with the Five Whys include the following:

- *Mutual trust and empowerment*: You should not be too critical of a mistake when it happens the first time, but ensure that the same mistake doesn't happen again.
- *Focus on the system level*: A flawed system would naturally generate many mistakes.
- *Face unpleasant truths*: There are times when this method will show unpleasant truths about your company. The effort that you put in to fix these issues from the start can make a big difference.
- *Start small and be as specific as you can*: You want to get these processes ingrained, so start out with the small issues and apply small solutions. You can put your focus on running the process regularly and involving as many people as you can.
- *Appoint a Five Whys master*: This will be the primary agent you use for change, so make sure that he or she has the right amount of authority needed to get things done. The master will be the one held accountable if the issues persist.

It is important that everyone on your team knows how to use the Five Whys method. This will ensure that unnecessary blame is never placed on anyone while also helping you solve the root problem as soon as possible. Without the Five Whys, not only would you be tempted to work with the easiest and first solution, but you would also miss the true root cause, leading to more issues in the long run. The Five Whys is a simple method, and it can be effective without taking up much time. What's more, it is going to save a lot of waste and avert problems down the line.

Chapter 8: The Steps You Need for a Lean Startup Business Plan

Starting a new Lean Startup can be an exciting time. You are ready to take that idea and bring it to the world – and hopefully make some profit off of it. You want to make sure that you do the steps the correctly. No one will go through a massive amount of work and invest so much time and money if he or she knows from the beginning that the idea will fail. This chapter is going to talk about the twelve basic steps to complete a Lean Startup to help you use them for your own business.

Starting the business idea

Many startups begin with much uncertainty. The principles that have long been used for management are not really suited to deal with the uncertainties of today, and they do not foster innovation. Starting a business in our current economy requires a Lean Startup business plan that can address the uncertainties that you, as an entrepreneur, are going to face.

Your business plan is going to help prepare you to manage the unexpected through a process of building, measuring, and learning. This process may seem redundant and boring to some, but it exists to help you avoid some of the common perils that startups face.

Advances in technology have improved our capabilities for production, but it is common for startups to doom themselves by not employing discipline or scientific approaches during the early stages. A Lean Startup business plan addresses all areas of your business from inception and beyond. This includes topics such as the conception and development of your product, the measurement of your progress, and the structuring of the business.

Defining the vision

Being able to cultivate entrepreneurship is a critical task of the senior management. They need to be geared to handle uncertain environments while the business is being developed, and the management needs to be able to guide a product from the idea stage to the production stage no matter what happens.

It is during the define stage in your business plan that you develop your vision. The strategy that you will implement is going to be a result of this vision, with the aim of furthering it along. This part of the business plan should include different elements like research on the marketplace you want to sell in and an assessment of the competition. Remember that the strategy that you implement in the beginning will likely be altered as you get measurements in and learn from them, but the vision is something that should always remain the same.

Learning

The learning stage is not going to stop after you've fully developed your business idea. You must also learn how to make this business idea work in the real world and how to move it out of the conceptual stage and turn it into a working product. You will need to understand which parts of the business plan are beneficial to your goals and which ones are not. This is also important when it comes to determining whether your company is going to do well or if it is going to fail.

Your goal here is to find any of the demonstrable truths about your business to reduce the uncertainties you'll encounter in the business world. These truths are going to help you govern your business and move it into the future.

This is a great opportunity for you to take some time and learn more about your company. If you have been running your company for a long time, it may be possible that you have gone on autopilot a little bit. You might not know everything that is going on, or you might not be up-to-date on the fact that there are better ways that you could run the business than the one you are doing now.

This is why you should take the time to learn. Learn how the market is doing right now, see what processes are being used by other companies, explore what new products and services you could offer, consider whether you can also implement new processes in your business, and take the time to learn more about Lean Startup and how it can help your business.

Experimenting with the business idea

It is impossible to learn anything if you do not take the time to experiment. Experimentation is more than just blindly tossing out some ideas when you are a startup and hoping that they work. When you experiment in business, it is going to involve testing your theories out in the real world. The theories that you choose to test are all going to come from your vision and what you learned about it in the previous section.

You can also take the time to test various parts of your business plan with some of your real customers to see whether the ideas are going to work or not. This kind of testing is useful because it is going to give you great information that can then be used to make concrete business decisions. This information is not something that you can get a hold of without doing practical experiments.

Now, the experiment can go one of two ways. It could end up confirming your beliefs. If this happens, then you can move forward with the idea with more certainty because you already have a good handle on the way the market works and what it demands. However, it is possible that the experiment won't produce the results that you want. This may mean that you need to change your business model and make adjustments based on the new data that you have. The key here is that you must be open to both conclusions and objectively incorporate new findings into your business plan.

Taking a leap of faith

If you want to move forward with your business plan, you'll need to take a leap of faith. The point of your experiment is to ensure that you are not taking that leap blindly. There are going to be two major unknowns in the world of innovation: whether you can build the product in the first place and whether or not there are customers out there who will want it.

To make your startup successful, the answer to both needs to be yes. All startups that end up successful could be seen as products of similar leaps of faith. Not taking these leaps can sometimes be seen as prudent, but at other times, it only means that you've missed out on a great opportunity for success.

Testing your idea

This is the point where you act on the second leap of faith and assume that you will have customers for your product. This is where you try to find them. Make sure that you have at least a basic version of the product for them to try out then closely gauge their reactions. You'll need a limited number of people to act as your test market.

In this stage, if the product is unsuccessful, you'll still not have wasted too many resources because you didn't produce at full scale. You can even split test with different versions of the product to help you get even more feedback. You can then assess the values that the customers gave to certain features based on the differences in each of your test groups. By being able to meet the demands of this small section of the market, you can get a much better idea of what the full marketplace will demand, preparing you better for a successful launch.

Measuring the results

This is where you measure out the results that you get from the testing above. You must have an effective method in place to help you analyze the data you've gathered during the testing phase. Figure out what your customers liked about a product, what they would like changed, whether they would purchase it if these changes were made, or whether they didn't like the product at all.

Having a good metric in place will make it easier for you to tell how your product did with the small test market.

Always take the time to measure the results you get. The testing that we have spent so much time talking about in this guidebook will be worthless if you don't spend any time studying the results that you get from it. If you do the testing properly, you will get feedback, suggestions, and more from your customers who got the chance to try out the product.

Now, there are different ways that you can measure how the testing works. You can offer a free trial for the product in exchange for some reviews from the customer. You can do focus groups to listen to what the customer thinks as they bring the product with them and use it. Depending on the product you are offering, there may be some other methods that you can use to measure your results and see what changes you need to make.

How and when to pivot

When it is time to pivot, it means that you need to make some changes to the strategy that you are using. However, that doesn't mean that you have to change the vision for your company. If your measurements come in negatively or if your testing shows that no one is willing to purchase the product, then you must adapt the vision so that it will be better able to meet the needs of your market.

To do this, you will need to take the measurements data you've acquired and use those to come up with a new approach. Your business must be agile enough to handle this big shift in methods any given time that your metrics dictate that this is necessary.

Not all startups will have to pivot with their products. Some may do just fine with making tweaks and changing up the product a little bit to make the customer happy. However, there are times when you must pivot to make your customers happy and ensure that they will actually go out and purchase that product.

To determine when a pivot needs to happen, you have to really listen to the information and the feedback that you get from your customers. The trick is that you need to recognize these signs and be willing to change your original idea. While you have probably grown attached to your product because of the time and money you have spent on it, your customers' views are still paramount.

Note, though, that while you must make this pivot if it is necessary, you also don't want to pivot and make big changes if a small one will do. You and your team can spend time looking through customer information and deciding what needs to happen after each test-run of the product.

Working with small batches

For a smaller startup, the speed of production is going to be a big factor. While you may feel that it is counterintuitive, producing in small batches is the more efficient method compared to producing in larger ones. Think of your batch as one step in production that you have to complete before you move forward. The larger the batch that you work with, the greater the risks of delays and the harder it will become to make any revisions if such is necessary.

Small batches are better because they allow for the whole process of building, testing, and measuring to be done much faster. The faster you can produce, the quicker you can discover any problems and fix them while efficiently using your resources. Small batches help your startup handle these issues more efficiently, and much faster than your big competitors can.

Sustaining growth

Of course, when you get started, you want to make sure that your business is going to grow. There are three main ways that your startup can see sustained growth:

- Having this growth occur because of the continual return of customers who were satisfied
- Word of mouth by the customers who use your products
- Advertising and sales done by the company

With the first option for growth, you want to make sure that the return of your satisfied customers is still exceeded by the new customers that you bring in. The second type of growth can be considered as viral growth, and the key thing that you will want to measure here is the number of new customers that each user of the product generates. Finally, with the third growth type, the important question to ask is whether the cost of your promotional efforts exceeds the benefit that you are getting. The measurements that you get from these are going to help you make good decisions to ensure that you generate good sustainable growth.

Sustained growth is crucial for any company. You want to make sure that your company is not only going to make it for this first product release but for a long time afterward. Many companies, both new and traditional, continuously try to innovate, provide new products for their customers, and keep their own place in the market. Learning how to sustain your growth and provide value for your customers into the future, not just for today, can help keep customers coming back.

Adapting to any new circumstances

Things are going to change in your chosen market. It doesn't matter how well you plan; there are going to be times when the market is going to morph or throw you curveballs. When this occurs, having a few methods in place so that you can adapt is going to be essential.

Entrepreneurs who are successful start out by adding this to their business plan. The key to adapting well is not foresight. There is no way for you to see into the future. Adapting is more about being flexible and being willing to abandon what doesn't work and replace it with something that does. Not only should you be prepared to enforce fundamental changes in your business, but you must also be prepared to do it quickly. Adapting to your altered circumstances is an essential factor that will determine whether the startup does well or fails.

The business world is always changing. No one can do the same things they did fifty years or more ago and not end up with a ton of waste or go under. You have to learn how to adapt to the circumstances that are going on in the market around you. It may be hard, and many people don't want to go through these changes, but it's necessary to help your business grow and keep earning more profits.

A culture of innovation

The importance of innovation is not something that is limited to startups. It is going to be beneficial to everyone, including companies that are large and established. The good news is that it is possible for you to create a new culture of innovation in any organization, whether you are brand new or have been in business for a long time. The nurturing and encouragement that can come from a management with an entrepreneurial attitude can help create a culture of innovation.

For your business to sustain this innovative culture, the methodology contained in your business plan must be something that you adopt and keep at for the long term. It needs to be your norm rather than something that you just do for a while and drop. If you only use this when the business first starts up, you are going to end up failing. However, if you make it a part of the natural culture of your business and work hard so that it will stick around for the long term, it is going to have a lasting impact on your Lean Startup.

Chapter 9: Steps to Get from Concept to Product with Lean Startup

When it comes to creating a new product, there are a few steps you will want to follow to ensure you are using the Lean Startup methodology correctly. If you can follow these steps, you should be able to rest assured knowing that your product, and your business, is going to be successful.

Here, we are going to take a look at a five-step design program that you can work on to help you get from the conception stage to the finished product stage. There are only five steps because the first who gets to market is the one who wins. Thus, the faster you can complete the product development cycle, the better the market share you can get. Of course, the product still needs to pique the interest of the consumer, or they are not going to purchase it.

Devote one step in the design process to one of the five workdays. The steps that you need to get done in these five days are as follows:

- Understand the problem
- Collaborative design
- Design and prototype
- Test and learn
- Iterate and refine

This method works because you'll be getting the right people together at the right time, and they are all going to put in the effort to make a difference. During this sprint, one of the most critical aspects is that everyone needs to be all in. Everyone must engage their complete attention and focus on the project at hand. When this happens, you will be amazed at the results.

Understand the problem

On your first day, you are going to work with your biggest group. The aim is to drill down on whatever problem you are trying to solve. You can spend time exploring your current customers and the journey they go through and use this story to help you discover their most common pain points.

During this time, you will want to start broad and work your way down to find the specific solutions that will work. You want to make sure that you have a big group for this day because then you'll have many voices talking and contributing. You want to make sure that you end your day with a clear agreement and consensus about the problem and that you will be free to tackle it throughout the rest of the five days.

You must know what the problem is before you go any further. If you are just randomly picking out a product to work on and not really understanding what problem you want to fix, either in your own company or for the customer, you aren't going to get very far. If you need to sit down and come up with a list of problems that you are currently facing (and every business will have a list, even ones that are doing well), that can help as well.

After you have a nice list of the things that you need to fix within your company, it is time to pick the one that is the most important. Sure, you will want to go through and fix all of them at some point, but right now, we need to focus on the main one. You can't design a product that the customers will enjoy and pay money for if it doesn't help them solve a problem. As a group, you must all sit down and figure out which problem you should be working on.

Collaborative design

The next step is when you work on your actual design. You will want to spend some time here talking about the journey of the user and how the different functions of that journey are going to flow from one point to the next. You will then be able to prioritize some of the features and put together a working map of what your finished product will look like.

During this day, you will want to work with a group that is smaller than the last, with perhaps fewer than ten people. For a startup, there will be different areas of the company that you would want to be represented, such as the C-level, front line, customer service, sales, marketing, legal, and product development. If you are working on an enterprise, you would want this day to be more design-, product-, and tech-focused.

Design and prototype

Now that you have reached this day, you will want to spend your time working on the actual creation of your product. You want to finish the day with a prototype that is up and running. Make sure that the prototype follows the design map that you made earlier and that you've spent time polishing it with research.

Remember that everything doesn't have to be perfect when you work on this prototype. You want to come up with a good product, and it needs to have the right parts in place so the customer can use it. You don't want it to fall apart or anything like that, either, but if it's not quite up to market standards during the first rounds, that's just fine.

After you come up with the prototype, you can then provide the sample to your customers and do some tests. You will learn a lot during this time, and that is when you can start fine-tuning it. You don't want to have a fine-tuned and finished product before you even start testing. There are bound to be things that the customers don't like or want you to change. As you go through more and more of these tests, you will then be able to further adjust and add the things that you want.

Test and learn

When you have your prototype ready, and in hand, you can spend this step working on some research. Real people are key if you want real responses. You can choose to go online and use the available resources to try and guess what the customers want, but you may end up with the wrong answers.

It is much better if you get real people to give you the responses that you need. Sure, it is possible to test out the product in a lab environment, but to really know how the customer will use the product on a daily basis and get a good idea of how they will respond to it, you must make sure that you get the product into the hands of a real user.

Hence, during this step, you'll want to go outside with the prototype, show off the product, and see how prospective customers like the product and how they would use it on a daily basis. Get a wide variety of customers who fit into your target audience to see the best results.

Iterate and refine

Once you have done all the other steps above, take the first iteration and refine it. You will want to make the changes based on what you had learned when you tested the product outside. You may have to go through this step a few times, as many as needed to get the results that you are looking for or until you have the perfect product.

Never go through and make any iterations or changes to your product without first testing it with your customer base. This is a big part of the Lean Startup process. You need to receive feedback from the customer to know what changes need to be made and whether or not your customers will respond the way that you want them to. It doesn't matter what changes you want to implement; they need to have data behind them during this process.

Remember that this system may take a bit longer for some products than for others. However, the fact that you can complete the process in five steps shows how easy it can be to use the Lean Startup system and see immediate results. With any product that you develop for your startup, you will be required to go through these five steps. Skipping one or not doing the iterations enough could result in you developing a product that none of your customers want.

Narrowing your focus to the design

As you go through the five steps listed above, it is important always to remember the goal that comes with your product statement. Keep the four questions below in mind to drive your product statement front and center at all times:

- What problem are you solving for the customer?
- Whom are you trying to help?
- How will you help?
- What exactly will you help your customers do?

If you can keep your focus on the project narrow while still being able to appeal to the core group of customers, you can increase your chances of producing a finished product that can add much value to your customers.

Chapter 10: Making More Sense of Customers

We have spent some time in this guidebook talking about the importance of your customers. Many startups will spend their time developing and creating a product and then put it on the market. Then, when it fails, they can't figure out what went wrong. The biggest problem is that you didn't include your customer into the mix.

There are a few tests that you can use to help make more sense of the customers you have or the potential customer that you hope to gain with your startup. These will help you design products and services that they are interested in to increase your profits. Some of the tests you can work with include the following:

Segmentation

The first test to consider is segmentation. The process of segmentation compares a set of data from your whole list of customers. You will need to choose the demographics that you want to work with and then have the system split up your customers, or your potential customers, into each one. You could divide them by age, lifestyle, gender, or location. If you are a startup, you may want to consider looking at customer data you can gather from the market that you plan to enter.

You can use this information to learn more about the buying behaviors of your customers. It can give you great insights into what types of products they would like, what things they won't like, and what you should add to the product to entice the customers better.

You'll want to divide your potential customer into a user segment to help you turn the data into something that is actionable. This analytics can do a lot to teach you about the customers you want to reach, but when all the information is put together as a whole, it is sometimes hard to draw conclusions you can use. Many markets are large, and this can present you with a ton of information. This can be confusing to look through, and since the information is so vast, it is easy to miss out on patterns and important data.

This is where the process of segmentation is going to come into play. When you learn how to filter the audience, you will then be better able to create a plan to make new products that serve them the most. Analytics can give you the information that you need, but segmentation can help you take action.

With segmentation, you don't want to only look at the data to learn more about your users; you also want to come up with data that you can act upon. Segmentation can help you with this. You can divide up the people in your customer base and learn how to advertise to them better than ever before.

Remember that not all customers are going to be the same. There are some who may purchase something just once, meaning they aren't regular customers. While it is still good to reach out to them, you want to learn who your regular audience is, what they respond to, and what keeps them loyal. This is going to ensure that you keep them coming back and that you can earn as much profit as possible.

At this point, you may be wondering how you should create a new segment of your potential customers. There are many different options that you may want to look into to help you create a segmentation. Before you get going with this, though, there is a process, or steps, that you should follow to create the right type of segmentation.

These steps include the following:

- What's the purpose of my segmentation? In what way do you want to use the segmentation? Do you want to use it to get more customers? Do you want to use it to make sure you are reducing waste in your company? Do you want to be able to understand your customers better so you can create a product that they really want? Being able to define the purpose of this segmentation can make it much easier for you to figure out how to segment the customers.

- Identify the variables that are the most important. There are many ways that you can segment your customers. You need to decide which variables you want to include in the segmentation to get the best results. Write these down in order of importance. You can use a Clustering or a Decision tree to help you out.

- Once you have listed out your variables, it is time to identify the granularity and the threshold for creating these new segments. You want to make sure that there are two to three levels that go under each variable. Of course, you may end up with more than this if the problem is more complex.

- Assign customers to each of the cells. This will give you a good idea about whether or not there is a fair distribution for your potential customers. If you don't see that the distribution is fair, you may need to tweak your thresholds a bit to make them work out. Keep going through these steps again until you get a fair distribution.

• Once you are done here, include the new segmentation that you have into the analysis you are doing. Take some time from here to analyze it at the segment level.

Cohort analysis

A cohort analysis is a great test to use because you can compare your data sites within a timeframe. With this test, there will be some differences in behavior between the times your customers made a purchase. You will see that the customers who came in during the free trial will be different compared to the ones who showed up when you first put the product on the market. Both of these groups are also different from the customers who are in the full-payment stage.

It is important to recognize which of your potential customers are going to fall into each of these timeframes. This is because when you look at them, it is easier to see which ones are going to come back and continue to be full-fledged customers. There are those who will try out a product just because it is free, but since they didn't put any investment into it, it is not likely that they will come back later and make a purchase. Those who came when the product was first launched, or who came in later on when the full-payment stage was on, were the ones who put in some investment; they are more likely to come back and make a purchase later on.

As a startup, you want to learn how to recognize which customers will come back and which ones are just there to try it out. This doesn't mean that the customers in the first group are not important. In fact, these are the exact customers you need to work with to learn more about your product and conduct your testing phases. However, you need to learn how to work with the customers who will make purchases, and who will come back more than once as well, to really help your new startup to grow.

A/B tests

The A/B test is going to be a great one for you to use, especially when you are still in the testing part of your new product. This allows you to examine an attribute between two choices. Let's say that you are creating a new product, but you are not sure which feature you want to add. You like both but would like to know which one the customers prefer. This is when you would bring in the A/B test to help you out.

You would introduce one product to the customer, but there is one attribute to each product version that is different. For example, Product A might be blue in color, and Product B might be red. You would then introduce both of these to the customers and see which one they responded to the best.

You could do a multivariate analysis, but this is a bit different, and it can cause some issues with your test. You may find that customers like both and want one of each. Or you may be confused about which change or feature they like the most. If you do this, make sure that you test out several changes against another group of changes.

There are a few things that you should make sure are in place to help you with one of these A/B tests. The things to remember are as follows:

- Know ahead of time what you are doing when you run the A/B test. What are you trying to test out and what changes are you going to have between the two products?

- The changes or features that you are testing with your customers need to be noticeable. If you make a change that is so minor or small that the customer can't even notice it, you won't get the reliable results that you want.

- It is best if you can pick just one variable to work with at a time. You can choose to do multivariate testing, but you may run into trouble when figuring out exactly what your customer likes or dislikes about the product.

- Your test should have some kind of statistical significance. This means that you must pick out a sample size that is big enough. This will help you know that the results are valid with little margin for error.

Chapter 11: Tips to Help You Run Your Lean Startup

The philosophy of Lean Startup has gained much popularity in the global startup industry. This is a great method to use because it is going to help new startups shorten their cycles for product development while also allocating time, effort, and money in the most effective manner possible. However, getting started with Lean Startup does take time and knowledge to do successfully. Let's take a look at some of the best tips that you can follow to learn how to properly run your Lean Startup, how to solve some of the biggest problems that may come up, and how to ensure that you will stay on the road to success with this methodology.

Make all assumptions explicit

Everyone on your team must be on the same page. They need to know what the goals of the startup are, who the customers are, and what the business model is. If people are all over the place on this, how are you supposed to run an efficient Lean Startup? You can make sure that everyone is on the same page here by having them fill out a Business Model Canvas and then comparing their results with yours.

Talk to your users

After you have made sure that everyone on your team has the same assumptions and that they are clear on all aspects of the business, it is time to test these assumptions to see how they work. You can spend time out of the office to get this done since this is where most of your customers will be. Talk to your customers about any problems that they have and how you can be there to help them solve these problems. Taking the time to test your assumptions with your users can really help you understand the value that you need your products to bring to the customers.

Build the MVP

Once you have a chance to talk to some potential customers and you figure out what they most want or need, it is time to focus on the MVP that you will create. If you recall, this is the most basic version of the product. You will add to this later on based on the feedback that you get from the customer, but you want to have at least the basics in place at this point.

You can then ship the MVP to your customers and ask if they are willing to provide feedback so that you can understand more about which product features you should build, improve, or get rid of entirely. This is valuable information that will help you continue developing the product and getting it ready to sell.

Accept that failure can and will happen

As a new startup, you have to learn to accept failure because you will soon find that most of your experiments are going to fail. If you don't have a thick skin that can handle this, you are going to run into problems in this industry. Instead of looking at failure in the traditional way, learn how to look at it as an expected outcome. You are going to fail, probably a few times with each experiment that you do, but you get to learn from it. And if you are able to learn from that failure, it basically turns into a success in the business world.

Plan out the persevere and pivot meetings ahead of time

You must spend some time meeting with other members of the team. This will help you keep looking at the data that you collect and discuss how the startup is doing at any given time. You should set up this meeting at least twice a month. These meetings don't have to last a long time, but it can help you ensure that the whole team is on the same side and that they are working towards the same goals to help the company. With these meetings, you can then make decisions about your company's next actions on the spot.

Always look at the data

It doesn't matter what your assumptions are. It doesn't matter how much you love a product or how badly you want to get it straight to market. It doesn't matter what others tell you. What you need to really concentrate on when working with the Lean Startup methodology is data. Data is going to be the lifeblood of any startup. You should always ask the question "How do I measure success?" Do I decide to use quantitative data or qualitative data? This often depends on the type of market you are trying to reach and on which metrics you decide are the most important. Remember that you shouldn't just blindly look at the data you have. Take the time to decide which metrics you want to use to measure what happened with the experiment.

Keep asking why

If you have a young child, you are most likely used to hearing the question "Why?" all the time. Kids always want to know why something behaves the way that it does, and even after you have answered the question fifty times, they will keep asking why. When it comes to using the Lean Startup method, you should revert back to childhood and always ask "Why?" One of the biggest things that you should find out about your experiments is the reason behind the customer's behavior. The Five Whys method discussed in this book will help you do this.

Ask yourself what you must learn about today to help you be successful tomorrow

Every morning when you get to the office, set some learning objectives that you want to work on for the day. You need to always remind yourself that this startup is an experiment, no matter which stage you are in. This is a stage where you are still figuring out what is going to work and what wouldn't for your business.

Focus on acquisition early on

You will quickly learn that the competition that you will face with your startup is going to be huge. There are only so many users in each market, and all the other companies in that market, from big traditional companies to many other startups, are all competing to get the same users and use the same channels to acquire these customers.

As a new startup, you may find that it is hard to build up acquisition channels that are scalable and effective. However, if you don't set these channels up, it is going to be really hard to make any sales and reach the customers you want. This is why you should put some focus on developing these channels as early into the journey as possible. Then, by the time you are ready to sell the product, you have some good and profitable ones ready to go.

Getting started with the Lean Startup method is one of the best things that you can do for a new business. When you use the tips mentioned above, you are more likely to do well with Lean Startup and get it to work for you.

Check out more books by James Edge

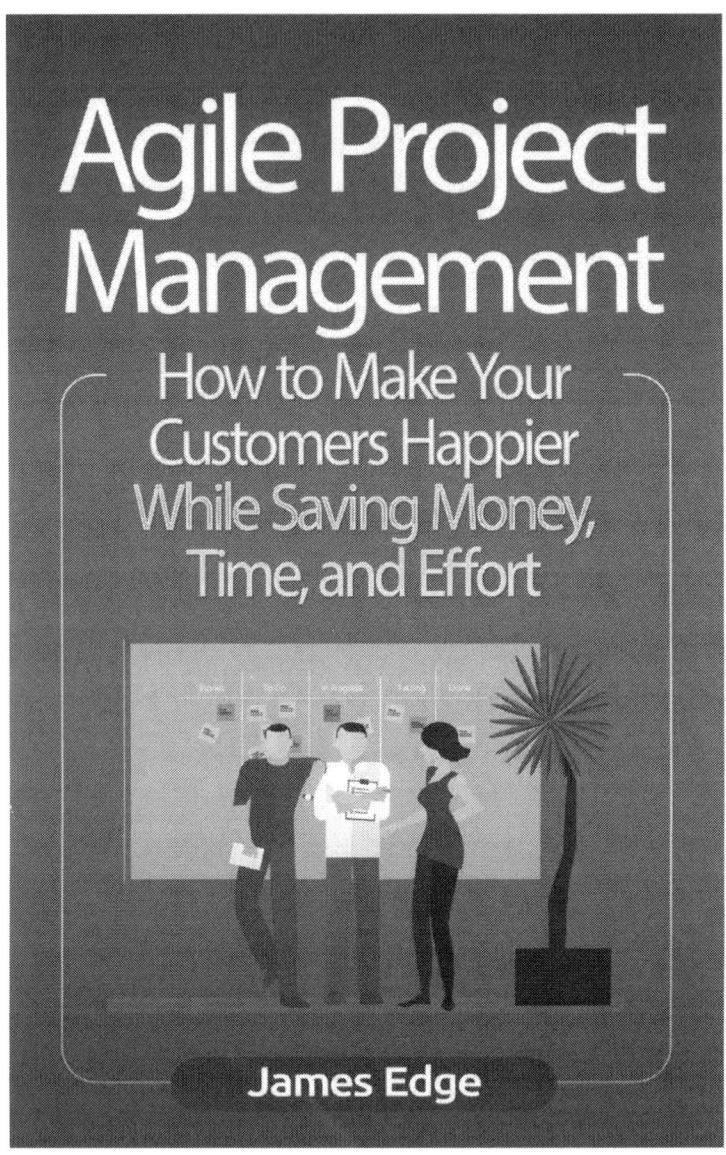

Printed in Great Britain
by Amazon